BOB CRIS

5TH Edition
All rights reserved

Copyright 1993
Library of Congress

NO DUPLICATION IN WHOLE OR IN PART

Crisp Publishing
668 N Coast Hwy
Suite 1349
Laguna Beach, CA 92651

Or

Bob Crisp
1515 N Federal Hwy
Suite 300
Boca Raton, FL 33432

email me at… bob@allaxismedia.com

Other Books by Bob Crisp

Feeding a Giant 2.0 (available online in ebook format or Audio CD, or as an MP3 format.

Poor Network Marketers Doing Better (Spring 2010)

How to Become a Millionaire in Network Marketing

Why Christians Should Always Do Network Marketing

CD Series "The Best of Bob Crisp"

Go to: www.gobobcrisp.com to order

Table of Contents

CHAPTER ONE..**11**
    My Story…Thank God for Larry

CHAPTER TWO..**23**
    Networking

CHAPTER THREE..**32**
    Cult or Culture? – The House Where the Giant Lives

CHAPTER FOUR..**41**
    A System That Works and Endures

CHAPTER FIVE..**58**
    The Art vs. The Science

CHAPTER SIX..**69**
    The Duplication Principle

CHAPTER SEVEN..**78**
    Who Shall Be The Greatest?

CHAPTER EIGHT..**90**
    The Ten Laws of Leadership

CHAPTER NINE..**100**
    A Giant's Heart

CHAPTER TEN..**108**
    Giant Power… Faith and Belief

CHAPTER ELEVEN..**116**
    The Giant's Friends…The Upline Powerline

CHAPTER TWELVE..**126**
    Symptoms and Diseases – The Real Causes of Failure

CHAPTER THIRTEEN...**136**
    How to Have Power-Packed Events!

CHAPTER FOURTEEN...**156**
    Recognition and Praise

CHAPTER FIFTEEN...**170**
    Perpetuity – Build it Once to Last

CHAPTER SIXTEEN..**185**
    Giant Living – Giant Life!

CHAPTER SEVENTEEN...**195**
    The Call of The Leader

CHAPTER EIGHTEEN..**212**
    The Fall of A Giant and The Road Back

Preface

This is the fifth edition of Raising a Giant... thanks to all who bought the previous editions and thank you for telling your friends. Please let everyone know there is a new and improved version available. This is 2009 and the internet is in full bloom. I am a believer that if you don't take change by the hand it will take you by the throat. In this edition I have attempted to make notations along the way to alert the reader to some ways the internet might affect your performance.

Bill Gates calls the internet the "Great equalizer" and I think he is right. Like fax machines, audio tapes, cell phones and three-way and conference calling... the internet has pushed mass communications and individual connections beyond anything before it. Today, if you use/adapt to the internet "emarketing" solutions you can almost assure yourself of success.

Like many of you, I waited for others to develop systems that could automate previously intimidating and time consuming activities... like calling a friend or acquaintance to "sell them" on buying a new product or getting into the latest and greatest networking deal on the planet.

A good emarketing campaign can offer a broad range of individuals a choice in what they want to hear about without feeling obligated or intimidated by a personal phone call. Used properly emarketing can informally "sort" those who will from those who won't. No sense irritating your negative brother-in-law even more... right?

Doing marketing without the internet would be like running a marathon with a hundred pound backpack on.

My advice is to seek out a forward thinking company and upline... and make sure that includes a great emarketing solution. Just because you don't know anything about it doesn't mean it won't work for you... find a mentor to teach you... that's what I did...now here's my story.

For the first 9 years of my career in networking I had the privilege of being sponsored into one of the largest network marketing companies in the world and into the largest leg of that company. Through no intelligence of my own I wound up in a position where I could be tutored by the best in the business. My former upline teachers have the largest and continually the most profitable and stable businesses in the industry.

Today I devote my time to many future giants of the industry and to promote the value of the networking concept wherever I go. In this book you will find an accumulation of ideas and concepts collected over the years. Most of them I admit I borrowed from others who have crossed my path. I don't claim to have all the answers for the older I become the more I am certain that life has allowed me to be here and discover the answers for myself as I uncover the great values possessed by others.

I make no claim to fame only that I have been involved directly in the building of a downline organization of

Bob Crisp - Raising a Giant 2.0

over 200,000 people with retail sales volume I believe to be in excess of one billion dollars at this writing.

As you will discover in the pages that follow, I am a believer in the team concept. No one can say "they alone" built a large organization. Instead, each organization is a collaborative effort. My sponsor could easily say that he, not me, is responsible for the fabulous growth of my direct downline business. I would have a hard time arguing the point for certainly, were it not for his patience and persistent effort, I would not be writing this book today. On the other hand, there were times when I found him to be more of a stumbling block than a stepping stone. I will explain why later in the book.

Were it not for mentors such as my first life insurance manager, the late Mr. Warren Gray, I would not have had the insight and wisdom to listen to the still small voice inside that whispered the encouraging words that led me on this long and winding road.

I believe that networking is life. The term "network marketing" is a redundancy. All marketing, in my opinion, is in some ways the result of networking and in these modern days of the internet we can magnify our own networking through social networks such as myspace.com, facebook.com, youtube.com, linkedin.com and many others. Their members number in the millions with a spider like web of connectivity.

The greatest form of free enterprise on the face of the planet is network marketing. No other industry offers everyone the opportunity to start with nothing but a dream and become financially free! It treats each person with equal disdain and respect. The stories of success and failure are endless.

    Each person is allowed the freedom to decide the amount of time, energy, belief, knowledge and commitment they are willing to place in their area of chosen endeavor. The failures, on average I believe to be no greater than those of any other industry. The real estate failure rate for agents is reported at over 95% in five years and the life insurance industry figures are even worse. Since in most network marketing companies you begin on a part-time basis, your chances for success over time seem to be improved.

    To begin most businesses you must invest large sums of money, quit your present occupation, train for a new field, work 80-90 hours a week and still risk an 85% failure rate for new businesses.

    In network marketing your risks will vary with the company you choose. Look for strong financial backing, good management, quality products competitively priced, and a decent pay plan. Stay away from fly-by-night far-fetched, heal-you-in-a-minute schemes with promises of overnight fame and fortune.

    Remember something that seems to be too good to be true usually is. However, I also caution on too much skepticism. Don't be afraid to take a chance. New companies offer a chance to the novice to be in on the ground floor. Playing it safe usually isn't. Just be wise. Don't fall for just anything. Look at the long term. Ask yourself if you really believe in the people who own the company. Do you have confidence in the product? Does there seem to be a real need for it?

Evaluate the players in your immediate upline. Are they veterans or are they beginners like you? What has been their track record? How many companies have they been with and did they move on or did the company fail?

Networking itself is an art form. In this book we will deal with this in depth. In the chapter on depth you will learn why it is important to work downline and how to evaluate things like ability and commitment early on. You will find yourself looking at friends and family differently. You will be challenged to look inward at yourself. Your skills with people will be exposed. You may not like what you discover. I didn't, but you can change and change you must.

This book is for beginners or people who have been around for a while and are frustrated with their lack of success. Maybe you have been given the wrong training or no training at all. Maybe your sponsor didn't know any more than you. Maybe like many you were left on your own with the admonition to "Go get some just like you" and you tried without success. (Later we will discuss how to evaluate a mentor)

This book is not for wishers, whiners, watchers or wienies. It is not for those who sit at home and watch television every night. This book is for the doers and dreamers, the ones who are never content with the status quo. This book is for the many that have what it takes and are looking for the right path to their highest dreams and ultimate aspirations. I am a dreamer and I am proud of it. Here, I will show you the path and hopefully shed some light

Bob Crisp - Raising a Giant 2.0

on your way. I can't make you successful. Only you can do that. I can give you the road map. You must make the journey. Good luck! If you persist you'll make it! I know it!!

You may reach me via email at bob@allaxismedia.com

Chapter One

My Story… Thank God for Larry

"There is no medicine for the life that fled"

My story begins as the son of a Baptist minister. Growing up in an environment where the ability to communicate was stressed everyday was quite a challenge. When you're the oldest son of a minister you're expected to become a preacher yourself. Those who know me today would probably say that the expectation was fulfilled.

I grew up in a not so affluent neighborhood in Southern California and developed an aggressive attitude early as a matter of survival. At 8 AM every morning at my high school they chain locked the six foot high gates that separated the students from the outside world, not to keep anyone out but to keep the inmates (students) in. The term "ghetto" hadn't made it to Los Angeles yet…except in an Elvis song of the same name.

I went to college on a half ministerial and half basketball Scholarship and left school late in my sophomore year. That ended my formal education. I moved to Oklahoma where my parents lived and started down the road to fame and fortune.

I joined the life insurance industry in 1969 and was a

spectacular failure. As a matter of fact in an agency of 50 agents I was number fifty every month. The only way I ever moved up was when someone quit. All of that changed one day when a highly successful agent with the Prudential insurance company came to speak to our agency at the monthly recognition banquet.

He said "If you're number fifty and you want to be number one I will tell you what to do," I leaned forward and paid close attention. He said, "If you're number fifty and you want to be number one you ought to go to this three day seminar" I said to myself, "I'm going to that seminar." He then said, "In California." I thought, "I'm not going to that seminar." He continued "It costs twelve hundred dollars." I reaffirmed my decision not to go to that seminar.

The speaker told us all why losers lose and winners win. He said winners do the things losers are unwilling to do. He went through all the excuses I was already conjuring up such as "too expensive, too far to go, I'll get the CDs later, the company should pay my way and others. I thought "the guy has been following me around taking notes." He had me pegged.

He convinced me that there was nothing more important to my future than to go to that seminar. I scraped together barely enough money to get me there and he was right, it changed my life. First of all because I let it change me. Secondly I needed to be changed. It changed my attitude about everything. I came home a different more determined person.

Bob Crisp - Raising a Giant 2.0

Lesson: The cost on NOT going may be more than any monetary cost you could pay. Most great things require sacrifice.

In six months my income went from under five hundred dollars per month to over seven thousand dollars! I can't tell you how excited I was! I led my agency in sales, I led my company in sales and I was only twenty six years old!

A few months before… a friend, Gary Hines, had given me a book called (Author Dr. David Swartz) 'The Magic of Thinking Big" that had set me on the road toward bigger things. I can't thank him enough for the thoughtfulness. A book that cost only $1.98 at the time, prepared me to accept the challenge to attend that crucial seminar.

You never know what it will be, a book here, a thought there, encouragement at an especially trying time, the little things all add up. For me, it was the training ground for the challenge of network marketing.

I started in the network marketing business in the mid-seventies. I was invited by a friend to meet one of his friends. He asked, "What are you doing this afternoon about three o'clock? Why don't you bring your wife and an appetite and come over to my house. We'll barbecue some hamburgers and I want to introduce you to a professional baseball player who serves on my board." I said, "Great we'll be there." (How could I have known that this small seemingly insignificant decision would change my life forever?

BOB CRISP - RAISING A GIANT 2.0

Lesson: Pay attention to the tiny threads that lead us to our next divine appointment with destiny.

That afternoon we drove to the friend's house and there as we drove up in the driveway was a large motor home. (I found out later it cost more than the house that I lived in.) That day I met a professional baseball player who was destined to show me an idea that changed my life. Bob Bolin, an established "big leaguer" had just gotten cut from the Boston Red Sox after winning the "Fireman of the Year" award as a relief pitcher the previous year. (So much for job security)

What I didn't know then, was that he had signed up in a network marketing company a few months earlier. Little did I know that day that the future was beginning to take a different turn for me.

I asked if I could take a look at his motor home. As we stepped into his motor home I noticed he had several copies of the book, "The Magic of Thinking Big" stacked on the small dinette set. Since I was familiar with the book I asked him why he had so many of them. He replied that he used it in his business. Having read the book, I knew that it must be a great business. I inquired what business he was in and he said, "I haven't got time to tell you now maybe we'll talk about it in detail at a later date."

Like many of you, I had been approached by the "curiosity" approach before, but this guy was so cool, I didn't even realize he was preparing me to see the plan in a more conducive environment.

BOB CRISP - RAISING A GIANT 2.0

Lesson: Always set the stage for the message you want to convey

We played golf, went fishing and hunting together, and occasionally as the subject came up I asked, "What are you doing to make money, Bob?" He would always answer with something obscure such as, "Well, I have a wholesale/retail business with about two thousand major suppliers. We'll discuss it sometime." Then he would change the subject. He was very protective. He baited me for about three or four weeks, and finally one day I got a telephone call and he said, "What are you and your wife doing next Tuesday night about eight o'clock?'

Lesson: Prepare the ground before you plant the seed

He said he and his wife Irene would like to come over and show us what they were doing to make money. Finally I was going to learn his secret. Shortly after eight o'clock the next Tuesday night, Bob and Irene showed up at our house with a yellow pad, a red felt tip pen, a strange looking case and a message of hope.

Jeremy and Julie, my twins, were about three months old and Candace, my other daughter was three years old. My wife kept getting up and down to go take care of the babies during their presentation. It took Bob and Irene three hours to explain the business opportunity to us.

That night I saw "The plan" for the first time. He drew some funny looking circles on his yellow pad, and then told me the name of the company. I could not believe it! This professional baseball player was selling soap and wanted me to sell soap too!

At the time, I was a "Professional Financial Planner" and thought I was doing pretty well. I was a member of the Million Dollar Club and was on the Board of Directors of Rotary. I could not imagine the people in my town ever finding out that I was doing one of those "pyramid" soap deals.

In great detail he explained to me the dynamics of passive income. He showed me the value of creating a recurrent, on-going income. I liked everything about the plan except the product and the company. With great patience he explained the value of "consumables" (travel is a consumable) to a program like theirs. For the first time I saw the concept of "Duplication." No one had ever bothered to take me that far. Soon they had won me over and I signed my first application.

I asked him how much it would cost me to get involved and how much of a time commitment it would be. He said, "It costs $36.75 to buy a sales kit and I'll be back next Tuesday night and you can invite some of your friends and we'll show them "The Plan Too!" I thought "How am I going to get out of this?"

That's how I got started. Probably your experience was much the same, nothing dramatic, nothing complicated, just straight forward friends talking to friends. I paid $36.75 for the ugliest looking sales kit you've ever seen, a black plastic vile looking thing.

BOB CRISP - RAISING A GIANT 2.0

The next morning after I saw "the plan," I had a new plan, a plan to get out of the soap business. I realized after sleeping on it that I had made a terrible mistake. I woke up the next morning and for the first time in my life I had to shave a soap salesman. That was a real awakening! So I came up with a game plan for getting out. Since my sponsor had told me I needed to have an event, I would just invite the two worst prospects I had. I invited an Optometrist, Dr. Rupe and my next door neighbor Kenny Robinson, a Senior Systems Analyst with a major oil company. I figured Kenny's so bashful he can't lead a silent prayer in church so he won't get in and Darrell Rupe, my other prospect, was a doctor and his wife would never let him do it.

The plan was simple my sponsor will come over, show the program and these two people will say no. As a matter of fact, they'll probably walk out in the middle of the event, and I'll turn to my sponsor and say that they were my best prospects, I guess I'm not any good at this and that would be the end of it.

Boy was I ever wrong! By the time my sponsor was halfway through the presentation, the doctor started moving out on the edge of the sofa, his eyes were as big around as saucers, and Kenny was sitting there taking notes feverishly. I noticed him nodding his head and I thought to myself this plan isn't working. My plan is going wrong. Bad wrong. But I'm still safe, I thought, he hasn't told them what it is yet. As soon as he tells them what it is, they'll be out the door. As soon as he told them what it was, they turned and looked at me and asked, "Are you in?" I looked at them and I said, "Yeah, It looks like I am now."

BOB CRISP - RAISING A GIANT 2.0

I was in…but just barely. Today I look back and think how slim the thread was that led me on this journey. (Tiny threads again) You never know just how close some of the best ones come to saying no. A smile, a warm greeting, being well dressed and courteous may be the difference for your best prospect. How would you like to miss someone like me or you because of some easy-to-fix subtle nuance? My sponsor was the difference for me.

That night I began to get excited again about the dreams and goals that I had for my life. I didn't realize the journey that I was on was going to lead me all over the world and was going to create an organization of over 200,000 people. I didn't know that the decision I made that night would take me around the world many times or that I would earn millions of dollars and have all the material things my family and I had barely dared to dream of.

However, success can be elusive. It didn't happen quickly at first. After six months in the business, our bonus check was only $3.63. True! I had to drive 22 miles one way to get it! As my sponsor handed me my check he said, "Guess where we're going next month? We're going to North Carolina to a family reunion." Since I didn't have any relatives in North Carolina, I couldn't imagine why I would have any interest in going. He explained that it wasn't a reunion of relatives but a reunion of business associates.

So off we went to North Carolina to attend our first major network marketing event. A Ford Van… five kids, diaper bags, formula, a skeptical wife… and a very small interest/intrigue with "The Business." It was there that I caught the vision of network marketing for myself. I saw something there that lit a fire in me then and the flame has

Bob Crisp - Raising a Giant 2.0

never gone out. I think when I die they're going to have to nail the lid shut on the casket to keep me from springing up in the middle of the funeral and saying, "Listen, have you guys seen 'The Plan' yet?" I hope the fire never goes out!

When we saw "The Plan," we lived in a house that we barely could afford and the payment was only $412.00 a month! Due to some bad business decisions, I was viewing the light at the end of the tunnel from a very short distance. It seemed like we owed everyone in town. Sound familiar? Our cars were worth less than we owed on them and bill collectors were getting unfriendly.

But after less than two years in the business we paid off every bill we had and paid cash for two new luxury cars and moved into a home twice as large as the one we lived in only a short time before. I never dreamed it could happen to me.

While I dabbled with the business the first six months my sponsor went on without me. He communicated with Darrel and Kenny and filled me in daily on what was happening in the soap world. I couldn't imagine how anyone of his stature could be so excited about something that turned me off so completely.

The family reunion changed my perspective on everything. Today I shudder to think what life would have been like without that event. Life has its turning points and that was certainly a big one for me. It wasn't easy. Friends and relatives thought I was crazy and folks at church thought I had gone off on a materialism tangent.

BOB CRISP - RAISING A GIANT 2.0

My work schedule was six nights a week every week for two years. I would show the plan to anything that breathed. I held as many events as I could day and night. When things went backward instead of forward - I pressed on. When others quit - I continued! I listened to every CDs I could get my hands on. I went to every event regardless of how far it was and never once complained about the cost of the learning process.

One seminar could save me two years of experience. That was the way I looked at it. I needed and expected results and I did everything necessary to get positive results. I never bargained with the price. I paid the price gladly.

Pat Matzdorf, once the world record holder in the high jump, was asked how he jumped so high. His answer, "I just throw my heart over the bar and the rest of me follows." That's what I did… I threw my heart into every minute of every day. Eighteen months later, I was a Diamond…thirty months to Double Diamond and forty months to Triple Diamond. At the time, that was an unheard of speed. My income went from zero to over one hundred thousand dollars per month and life was more fulfilling than I had ever dreamed possible.

I had a friend in my church named Larry that I showed the plan to who just laughed at me. This was one of those people who "really needed it" who was living on welfare and eking out a bare existence. Larry didn't smile and say "No thanks. No!" Larry laughed!

Three years later, the company sent me and my wife an invitation to the company's Executive Diamond Council in Europe. Two first class airplane tickets were in the envelope and we were so excited! As the plane was descending through the clouds over Geneva, Switzerland, we could see the Alps. We looked down and saw cattle grazing in the fields below and could imagine the sound of the bells around their necks. I leaned over and whispered in my wife's ear, "I wonder what Larry's doing today"!

Larry was a big part of my success because when I would get a little tired or slightly discouraged, I would think of him and remember that he said it wouldn't work or that I couldn't do it. Maybe you'll have a Larry in your life too. Most of us do. Thank God for Larry.

Lesson: Don't let the turkeys get you down… if they were smart they'd be rich…turn you negatives into motivation

Looking back today, I realize that I am evidence that "The System" works…a system that works is essential. I know the system well for I am the fruit of that system.

Note: What most companies' call a "System" is really nothing more than a "Pattern" and while there is always a pattern within a system the pattern itself is nothing more than a component of a real system.

But first, to have a system that works, you must have a company that works. The company must have a well defined culture combining people with ability with dynamic and honest leadership who have compassion and a thorough understanding of the processes of being and becoming a leader.

The Larry's of the world are willing to accept life as it comes to them. Like the proverbial "sheep" they wait for the shepherd to lead them to the next field. To be a true giant one must be willing to step out from the flock and be different.

Leaders are perhaps the loneliest people in the world at times but they would have it no other way. Leaders take solace in knowing that what they are doing is important and makes a difference in the world. Becoming a giant wasn't nearly as difficult as remaining one.

Chapter Two

Networking

"The secret to success in life is for a man to ready for his opportunity when it comes." -- Benjamin Disraeli

While this book is not about religion, it is important to the context of the subject matter to establish some facts about networking and its origins. One needs only to go back some 2000 years to the birth of Christianity to begin to see the natural beginnings of networking. Christ met his disciples in small groups or one at a time. He chose twelve. They were all from different backgrounds and professions... a fisherman or two, a scholar, a teacher, a tax collector, an accountant. His message to them was a simple one......" Go and tell them about me…bring them to me and I will tell them a story that will change them forever" (apologies to the King James Version).

Networking is people-to-people communication. Can you imagine that someone actually bought the first telephone? Why? Who were they going to call? A professional such as a doctor or lawyer knows the value of networking and immediately upon establishing a practice joins the Rotary, Kiwanis, Lions or Chamber of Commerce. We would think nothing of recommending our hairdresser or barber or a favorite restaurant or church to a friend. We talk about movies we like and stores we shop in. We ask others about vacation spots and even call 1-800- DENTIST to find a dentist when we move into a new area.

Yet strangely enough, many people reject network marketing as too overt, too pushy or too crass an expression of this principle. The irony here is that anyone could ever believe any form of networking to be unworthy if it accomplishes an honorable and desirable end.

Why is there so much controversy over the network marketing industry? Why do so many feel so strongly about the companies and products? I believe it is because network marketing does to us what organized religion and politics do to us-it challenges our belief system.

Network marketing is about people. It is about confronting ourselves, about fear, and about how we stack up in this world. In everyday jobs no one points out that they are doing better than we are. They let us drift in our own space without making us feel too insecure. Network marketing, through recognition systems and pay plans, lets us know that we can do more, that if we do more we can have more or be more. The people around us move up to higher levels. If we don't, it is obvious to everyone.

The typical work-a-day world doesn't care if we are lazy couch potatoes. The work-a-day world encourages boredom and shiftlessness. It says "Don't step out from the crowd, if you do you might fail." (Not you might succeed).

Success to many is an affront, an offense of the highest order. Many of us are victims of an on-going human conspiracy... A conspiracy that reaches to every home, church, school, and business in America. A conspiracy which condones average behavior, eulogizes corruption and crime, uplifts athletes to superstar status giving them power and influence over society and lets the real heroes...the doctors and nurses, school teachers and ministers, others whose lives make everyone else's more vibrant and alive, go un-heralded and unrecognized.

Network marketing singles people out, people like you and me, for special accolades and acknowledges when we do something great. It pays us beyond our wildest dreams whether or not we can throw a fastball or hit a curve ball. Network marketing is the only real arena where we can test ourselves against the negative influences and win again and again.

Everyone has a network. A recent newspaper article on the subject quoted a well known 60's radical turned network marketing guru, Jerry Rubin as saying, "The least networked person in
America is no more than seven phone calls from the White House."

Your network may not be as developed as someone else's, but never the less you have a substantial network. To really understand the root cause of success or failure in network marketing you must analyze your network and the relationship you have with it.

For example, if you are a Boy Scout troop leader, pastor, president of the civic club or are in a profession such as real estate, life insurance, show business or some other area of sales and marketing, you may have a really well developed network with a large degree of credibility already established. On the other hand, if you have been on the sidelines watching the little league or civic club or church develop, you may have a dormant or stagnant network that you are going to have to invest some time in developing.

Note: The internet and the use of social networking sites has allowed even the shyest person to network around the world from the safety of home base.

To understand what you must do, you have to spend some serious time in personal development. Skills with people take some time to develop. You may never be a dynamic speaker, a stage entertainer or the life of the party, but you must learn to communicate with your fellow man. If you don't, network marketing is not for you.

This is a business which requires salesmanship and statesmanship. It is a business that will stretch you beyond any former limits. The joy of working with people can only be exceeded by the extreme exasperation of working with the same people.

A network then is made up of the people you know and will meet and the people they know and will meet. To be successful, we must establish some facts and principles that we can agree on in our relationships with these people.

First, everybody is entitled to their own opinion. Opinions are like noses, everyone has one. In the world of network marketing there are those who have a prejudicial view. They believe by nature all network marketing companies are a fraud and a scam. It is a very small minority but usually a very vocal one. Then there are the skeptics and cynics. These are the ones who believe that it works if you are at the top. They never stop to consider that this is a fact of life at their company too. Then there are the open-minded persons or those that have not decided one way or the other about network marketing. This third group far out numbers the other two combined.

The key here is to sift through the first two groups to find the third group. Remember, no matter what business you choose, there will always be the dooms-dayers and naysayers who will tell you it won't work.

Success in networking is not making value judgments on what others do. It lies not in the concept of what you can do for me but rather in what I can do for you. Imagine having met someone at an office party or civic function and calling them a few days later and simply reintroducing yourself and asking the simple question "How can I help you?" The response would usually be one of considerable surprise. After all, how many times has a new acquaintance of yours called and asked how they could help you? The key then to initial success in networking is to reverse the usual what can you do for me idea and replace it with what can I do for you?

You will be surprised at the result. Soon they will ask the same question of you. You will have a help team that will propel you to new heights. You will wonder why you never thought of this amazingly simple formula yourself. Doesn't it irritate you just a bit to think that you spent so much time in the dark on this simple idea?

Successful networking simply put is based on what you can do for someone else rather than what they can do for you. All networking is a value exchange - how I can make your job easier, life richer and more stress free, and your business more successful. The unwritten law of exchange is how you can help my life in the same areas.

Remember, The Master Teacher said, "Whatever you would have them do unto you do unto them likewise." It is a strange but simple truth. Network marketing is based on a principle that is over 2000 years old and just as applicable today as ever, "each one reach one and teach one to reach one."

Lesson:

The principles of success are timeless. They know no boundaries, limits or prejudice. What you sow you reap. Sure there are floods, droughts, and pests that destroy our crops from time to time, but these things average out over time when you are dedicated to the long term. Disaster could easily take your first crop as well as the third one, but if you sow consistently, and cultivate constantly, you will reap a great reward!

Most of us give up opportunity for security. We have bought into the idea that working for someone else somehow makes our position in life more secure. The fact is that security is a myth. Helen Keller said it best, "Security for the most part is a superstition. It does not exist in nature, nor do the children of men as a whole, experience it. Avoiding danger is no safer in the long run, than outright exposure. Life is either a daring adventure or nothing at all." Dr. David Viscott, a popular television call-in host and psychiatrist, and author of a book called "Risking" a few years back says, "If you have no anxiety, the risk you face is probably not worthy of you. Only the risks you have outgrown don't frighten you. If you create a life that is always comfortable, always without risk, you have only created a fool's paradise."

The challenge that network marketing offers is opportunity itself. It confronts us with an open door and challenges us to take a chance on ourselves. Step out and trade what exists for what might be. It is a journey worth making. You too can become a giant. Success is a personal choice--so is failure and mediocrity. Acquiring success oriented behavior comes through the observation of achievers and the principles that guide them.

When we come face to face with our dreams, we can only begin with what we have at that moment. This is a negative experience for those who believe that "the jig is up" that "the party is over" and has no choice but to accept his or her fate. Folk wisdom teaches that only those who have inherited wealth or a special talent or gift can go to the top. Barring accident or tragedy what we want is what we get.

At this point, I use the word want in its strongest sense. For the achiever whose personal interest depends on his or her efforts and not accident or luck, the word implies a variety of appropriate responses. Not only do I desire to reach my goal, but I will focus my thoughts on it; I will learn from persons who have achieved the goals I value; I will work to reach my goal; I will believe in my ability; I will learn from adversity; and I will never quit. None of these attitudes depends on luck, inherited wealth, or special talents, but personal choice.

Network marketing is an industry that allows you choices. How much do you want to make? How much do you want to work? What do you want to become? It's your choice. Networking implies connectedness. Connecting with others is the way to learn and to grow. Like getting better at playing the piano, tennis, golf, or acting, the better your teacher the better your education and learning experience will be.(Vital in an era of "Intellectual Distribution")

Network marketing flows from an exciting blend of art and science, of soul and technique. I have made it my life's work to understand the science of network marketing and personal achievement. But it is the art form that I love. You must practice the science with an artistic flair to achieve maximum results. The art form can be learned. By watching the painter we can feel his moods and see through his eyes the picture that is yet to be painted on the canvas.

You too can develop an eye for talent. You too can become sensitive to the harmonies of life. The art form is the music, the science is the words. Just as the words and the music must match, so must the art coincide with the science. Networking is as much science as art. Knowing when to turn on the after burners and light the fire is an art, knowing how to do it is the science.

"The girl that can't dance…says the band can't play."

Many reject the application of the art form as too difficult, hokey or corny. But as most corporate moguls will tell you, it isn't so much what you know but who you know that counts. Get to know everyone you meet as well as time and circumstances will permit. Don't allow an opportunity to pass without handing out a business card and collecting one.

BOB CRISP - RAISING A GIANT 2.0

From grocery store check-out lines to cocktail parties, go with one thing in mind...... meet as many new people as possible and don't forget to follow-up with a note or call within a few days.

Start building your new network today. Your future depends entirely on it. To change your destiny, change your network. *Five years from today your income will be the average of your five best friends.* Twenty years ago when I first heard this statement I wrote down the names of my five best friends and beside their names I wrote what I thought they earned the year before. I looked at the list and said to myself "I gotta get some new friends." It's true. If you run with winners you'll become a winner. If you run with average people you'll be about average. And who in their right mind even considers the other alternative?

In conclusion, as you read the following chapters, please remember you are the missing link in this equation. The laws of the universe apply to you as it does to me and all who live here. You alone are the key. Study these principles, practice them and win. Ignore them, compromise them, bend them in any way and you will suffer the consequences.

Network marketing is fun and rewarding. It is also frustrating and inconvenient. But most of all, it is a vehicle that can take you to the tallest mountain and make all your dreams become a reality.

Chapter Three

Cult or Culture? - The House Where the Giant Lives

"And he will be like a tree firmly planted by streams of living water, Which yields its fruit in its season, And its leaf does not wither; And in whatever he does, he prospers." -- Psalm 1: 2-3

Once upon a time there was a very wealthy man who had a daughter whom he loved very much. The daughter fell in love and became engaged to a young ambitious home builder. The father summoned the young struggling builder to his office one day and asked him to find the most beautiful property in the area to build a house for him. He told his future son-in-law it was to be a surprise gift for his wife and not to divulge the project even to his own daughter. He said the builder could use his own discretion in choosing the materials but that they were to be the best money could buy.

The shrewd young man cut corners at every turn. Instead of buying a beautiful lot on a hill with trees and a view he bought a cheap unimaginative site for the home. He chiseled on everything... the carpets, the fixtures, the kitchen. He used substandard materials in the frame, roof and foundation. He billed his future father-in-law for the most expensive while providing shabby and inferior amenities.

BOB CRISP - RAISING A GIANT 2.0

The day came when the home was completed and the young man went to give the keys to his fiancé's father. The father asked the young man "Is this a truly fine home?" The young builder lied "Yes sir, the very best." The father began to weep as he told how much he loved his daughter and how much he would miss her. He said "I've always wanted to give her a beautiful new home for her wedding and I knew if I told you the home was for you it might mean cutting corners or saving money and I wanted you and my daughter to have a really fine home. And with that he put the keys to the new house into the young man's hands and said "It's your house, you built it for you."

What do you want to have when your home is complete? Many network marketing companies disregard this issue in the founding of their businesses. They may have a business plan to take care of financial concerns for the administration, marketing, or products, but they ignore the "kind of company" they hope to be. A business plan without a corporate philosophy and mission statement is impotent and nearly worthless.

No one in their right mind would ask a contractor to build them a house without a set of drawings or blueprints nor would a prudent investor start out with a network marketing company without a true vision of what he or she expected the outcome to be. Your concern here is to determine what you think the company's culture is and to understand your upline's interpretation of that culture.

The issue of corporate vision revolves around the company culture. Does your company simply allow it to evolve or is there a master plan shaping it from the beginning? It would be discouraging to get down the road a

Bob Crisp - Raising a Giant 2.0

few months and find that the people you are working with have no ethics or long term vision. The mission statement and vision should be obvious and the actions of the top brass should match the statement.

There should be no difference between the perception and the reality of ethics. Installing a culture after the fact is much like trying to balance the wheels of a car while the car sails down the highway at eighty miles an hour.

You must decide at the start what your idea of the company culture is. You should then promote that culture within your organization. If you cannot agree with the culture, then you are in the wrong business! Your integrity and reputation are at stake and the ideals embodied in the corporate statement of ethics and practiced at the highest levels in the field is what will determine the reaction of your friends and family to the business you are in. I would add that the "perception" of ethics and the "reality" should match.

An airplane leaving Los Angeles and heading for Miami would miss its target by hundreds of miles if the compass setting were only a degree or two off at the beginning. The same is true of a network marketing company. Unless we begin with the proper end in mind we are certain to suffer an ignominious defeat.

As a distributor surround yourself with people whose ideals, goals, ethics and style fit with your own. In a network marketing company the first distributors in will usually shape the integrity, tone and pace of the company.

Recently watching a television interview with Mr. Kelleher, a Co- founder and chairman of Southwest Airlines, one of the only U.S. airlines to turn a profit last year, I was shocked to hear him say that the reason for his companies' success is "psychic-satisfaction." Psychic-satisfaction? I was perplexed too. He added that the people at Southwest Airlines all have the attitude of "We're the best because we give our best." In other words, Mr. Kelleher was saying the culture of our company is, "Together we can do it," as opposed to the every man for himself attitude that prevails in most companies today.

Sam Walton, the deceased founder of Wal-Mart stores and one of the wealthiest men in the world, used to have early morning sales events in rural stores where the first order of business was a cheer he would lead while standing on a folding chair in the aisle. He would shout "Give me a W" and so on until the incredulous if not enthusiastic clerks, stock boys and managers had spelled out Wal-Mart and were throwing their fists in the air and shouting "Wal-Mart, Wal-Mart, Wal-Mart" at the top of their lungs.

What Sam Walton, Herb Kelleher and all successful business people know, is that the company culture is vital to the long term success of the business.

Individuals need to feel secure in the knowledge that they are with a "top flight outfit." They need to feel the power of being a part of something bigger than themselves. They need the psychological reinforcement that their cohorts and associates are truly interested in their individual success.

People will only follow those who are obsessed with high goals and dreams. Certainly Donald Trump, Mary Kay Ash of Mary Kay Cosmetics, Rich DeVos of Amway, Ross

Bob Crisp - Raising a Giant 2.0

Perot with his EDS group and a host of others would attest to the fact that the culture of the company is the heart and soul of the company.

History is replete with those whose obsessions have advanced civilization. Madame Curie, Jonas Salk, Thomas Edison, Tom Watson and others are famous names that come to mind when we think of the positive advancements that have come through compassionate obsessive behavior.

However, the challenge with network marketing has been that the typical person/distributor has no specific passion or dream that drives them along. This problem or dilemma may only be resolved with a leadership development program that is consistent with the company's culture. Con-artists and crooks won't remain in a program for long where ethics and principles are practiced and enforced.

Companies whose message is impotent and unclear are doomed to failure regardless of how good their product or how well financed they may be. Likewise, distributor groups will fade away quickly when no higher power lies behind the objectives of the individuals that make up the group. The realization that you must become a cheerleader, a protagonist and a motivator is one that has brought many to the conclusion that network marketing is just not for them.

Ross Perot is often depicted by many who worked for him at EDS as "a maniac on a mission." No wonder so many people were touting him for President of the United States.

BOB CRISP - RAISING A GIANT 2.0

In business when we shout and applaud at sales rallies or business gatherings, we are usually criticized for being a cult. When we become obsessed with success and financial well-being, we are targeted as materialistic or greedy by those whose own goals do not drive them beyond the daily routine. These generalizations are unwarranted for the most part and should be ignored.

The same critics would think nothing of standing and cheering until they were hoarse at an athletic event. Society, it seems, cannot bring itself to applaud for those who are rising out of the ranks of ordinary daily life-the truck drivers, school teachers, nurses, insurance and real estate agents, bank tellers, engineers, and computer programmers who enter network marketing and get excited about the opportunity for financial freedom.

The absence of a severe understanding of the role of a company culture is apparent in companies when they shade the role of the distributor and put the spotlight on themselves. As you will see in the chapter on recognition and praise the "cocooning effect" will cease only when people feel validated and safe in the new environment created by you, your upline and your company. A good case in point is Amway.

Amway, the largest network marketing company in the U.S.A. is nearly a 4 billion dollar a year company. Its founders, Jay Van Andel (deceased) and Rich DeVos, are wealthy beyond all speculation. Their success stems, in my view, from the willingness to put the proper perspective on the elements of the building of a successful business.

BOB CRISP - RAISING A GIANT 2.0

Dexter Yager, the largest and most successful network marketer in the world, resides in Charlotte, North Carolina. I happened to be in his downline during my initial foray into the network marketing world. He has been accused of running a quasi-religious order rather than a business. I admit there were times when I question the wisdom of the activities which take place at some of his events, but I believe in results. Not that the end always justifies the means. However, I think the bottom line is the basis from which each of us must evaluate the process.

The results are astounding! Amway has over 2 million distributors worldwide, and their annual product sales are in excess of 7 billion dollars! They hold the largest sales events anywhere in the world year in and year out.

Cult or culture? The difference, I believe, lies in the following: a cult will take away your will and replace it with their will; a cult removes individual incentives and rewards. Amway Corporation and Dexter Yager in particular, emphasize the dignity of personal achievement and stress the importance of individual recognition. So much so that over half of the time at events are devoted to nothing but individual recognition!

Many times I've had the pleasure of standing at the head of the Champs- Elysees in Paris where you will find The Arch de Triomphe and marvel at the wisdom of one of the world's greatest leaders Napoleon. On the Arch he listed and depicted the names of many of his generals. Not only did he honor the men who fought with him he knew that these men would bring their sons to see this magnificent monument to their accomplishments. He knew that one day he'd need to raise another army of strong, young, brave warriors and that the sons of those he recognized on the monument would volunteer for battle so that one day their names might be on a similar monument… I guess that is why he said…

"Give me enough medals, and I'll win any war"

— **Napoleon**

In the world there are many who would prey on the unsuspecting, the young and the old. There are plenty of evil people willing to sell their morality and integrity for a dollar. It would be unfair to characterize all network marketing people with this characterization. Just as it would be wrong to characterize all government officials by the ones who are on the take or abuse their positions of power.

The culture of a network marketing company is a statement of its morality and commitment to people. It embodies the good that all mankind seeks and provides a way to better ourselves and feel good about our labors. It can be no better than it's most vociferous and dedicated leaders. It requires a massive message, one that everyone can relate to.

Men and women everywhere are looking for something that will give their lives meaning and prosperity. As I said in the preface, network marketing treats us all alike with equal parts of respect and disdain. The culture and image of you and your company are shaped by the message and the messenger. Isn't it time to stand up and be counted? Isn't it time to make a mark on the world you live in? Isn't it about time you stepped out of the background and into the foreground? Why not reach for the stars?

So, if you have a bell to ring, stand up and ring it! If you have a song to sing, lift your voice to the sky and sing it! If you have a dream, don't be afraid to dream it. In doing so you establish a forward motion that others will follow. We are not in this thing called life alone. We have a right and a responsibility to become and do more. The culture of your company should shout integrity and respect for the individual. If it doesn't, find one that does.

Chapter Four

A System That Works and Endures

A "system" defined by Webster... 1) A group of interacting, interrelated, or interdependent elements forming a complex whole. 2) a set of facts, rules, etc. , arranged to show a plan. 3) a method or plan. 4) an established orderly way of doing something. 5) the body or a number of bodily organs functioning as a unit.

When I first entered network marketing I heard the term "The System." For the longest time I can honestly say that I didn't understand what "The System" was. I couldn't see it, taste it, touch it or hear it. It was elusive to me.

I would hear leaders in my upline say "Those people are not plugged in to "The System." But I didn't know how they differed from those who were plugged in.

After many years of network marketing experience I began to understand the vital patterns that need to develop to keep a network marketing company and its field leadership on track. I realize today how the subtle shifts and changes can move the organization off course. Today I realize that "The System" is the entire picture of what we do. Taken in pieces it is not a system at all just unrelated individual parts.

To build a giant network marketing business I address the elements of "The System" three distinct ways ...

A. Put them in

B. Keep them in

C. Move them along

These three areas are distinctly different. A successful system will do all three. Systems which promote only two of the three will break down in the long run. The system is like a puzzle - a jig saw puzzle. We don't do much jig saw puzzling these days but a jigsaw puzzle usually consists of several thousand pieces which when put together combine to look exactly like the picture on the puzzle box. You've probably done a jig saw puzzle but in case you've led a deprived life and have had to rely on TV and Nintendo instead, let me spell it out for you.

Jig saw puzzles are great family entertainment. As children, my brother and I never had much TV. We always had puzzles to put together. We'd spend our evening hours after homework putting puzzles together. My mother would pop some popcorn and if we were lucky we would get a coke to drink along with it and the entire family would stand around a card table and look for pieces to the puzzle.

It was a wonderful time of bonding and communication. We'd be so pleased with ourselves when we found a piece that everyone else had been looking for.

There's a system to putting a puzzle together. The puzzle is poured out on a table and the first thing you do is

BOB CRISP - RAISING A GIANT 2.0

turn all the pieces so that the shiny or colored side is up. Then you separate the border pieces, the ones with a straight edge first. We would take the pieces to the puzzle which are the easiest to identify and most obvious, and put them together to form the border or frame for the picture. This is a good recommendation for building your business as well.

Put the things into motion that are obvious first, such as making prospect lists and setting up events or home parties and learning basic contacting and inviting techniques. I discuss these concepts in detail in my basic Step One Guide and my CD "I Love The Phone" to help you.

The picture you have of your business is like the picture of the puzzle you saw on the box. You selected the result when you bought the puzzle. Now all you have to do is search for the pieces. You know they're all there! The question is will you be diligent in finding them? How much time will you devote each day to your puzzle?

There are times when you can stand over a puzzle and you can't seem to find a piece of the puzzle that fits. You can stand there for hours and not put one piece in the puzzle. Nothing seems to fit, and you swear the manufacturer must have left some pieces out. You walk away for a while and when you come back to the table you immediately find some pieces that fit. (The thing I always hated was when someone else walked up to the table after I stood there for an hour and a half frustrated over this puzzle, and says "Oh, that one goes right there").

Why? It took someone with a different perspective. You may have had to go out, take a break and come back with a different view, for you to be able to see how it fits for you. "The System" is an orderly way of doing things. Like the puzzle, this system makes it a complete picture, not a jumbled up box of unrelated pieces but a "complex whole."

"The System" is the methods and means by which independent distributors work together to form a unified program to do the following things:

1. Have events
2. Sell products
3. Recruit new distributors
4. Promote unity and personal growth
5. Support one another
6. Provide for perpetuity.
7. Protect the business from inside and outside negative influences
8. Promote harmony within the community at large
9. Develop individual leaders that among other things understand…

Leadership Topics

A. How to use the "system" in recruiting
B. How to secure your business before "pulling out"
C. Spreading the risk geographically
D. Developing and implementing recruiting and selling campaigns

The System's Events and Recognition programs all are important pieces to your business puzzle. They also create a bench mark for action and attitudes that you need to remind you of where you are going. The "Event System" is a modern form of Napoleon's Arch.

A friend of mine was doing a seminar one day and asked the audience what the most important part on the car was? Some in the audience guessed the carburetor, others the ignition, others the gasoline, still others the tires or steering wheel. My friend simply said, "The most important part of the car is the part that's missing"

The challenge with many network marketing businesses is that the pieces to the puzzle are obscure or simply missing altogether. In a healthy network marketing company the pieces to the puzzle are all there if you'll stick around long enough to find them. They may need to be turned over, the straight edges may need to be more clearly defined, or they may need someone with a different and new perspective to bring a fresh new focus to the table.

When you were born, you were given all the right body parts you were going to need as you grew up. You didn't have to wait until you were a year old to have your parents take you back to the hospital to have your legs and arms sewn on so you could walk and feed yourself. We are each given the tools to do the job and we are allowed to discover for ourselves how to use them. In a healthy organization all the necessary pieces will be there.

Without a dynamic leadership development program or recognition system, or a communication schematic the organization will remain confused and fragmented.

Dr. Robert Schuller, noted author and lecturer, says, "A commitment to continuity produces emotional stability."

BOB CRISP - RAISING A GIANT 2.0

Life in general is constantly changing. Stability and continuity are elusive. A strong organization stresses elements which give the members a sense of security and emotional stability. This produces the environment for long term growth and personal development.

Remember, not all the distributors in your downline are equal. Therefore you must create multiple growth tracks and development programs to accommodate a wide variety of needs.

The Group vs. My Group

The System revolves around the issue of "The Group vs. "My Group." The Group is the entire body of those working together. This may represent the entire company or simply a large arm or "leg" of the company. The Group is this entire body, a whole, not a part, not an arm or a leg but the whole body of people who make up a group of people who find synergy in their goals, methods and means of obtaining those objectives.

My Group, obviously is, then, the people that are only in my downline. The most common feeling prevalent in network marketing is to put your own group first. It is common to hear "If you're in my downline, I'll pay attention to you but only if I'm making money off you." I've even heard people advise distributors in other groups to "Drop out and transfer to MY group so I can help you." This kind of thing is destructive to the unity and culture of an organization of any kind. In network marketing it is totally devastating.

The "line-of-sponsorship" is a sacred component of any network. It is the only thing that differentiates us from

BOB CRISP - RAISING A GIANT 2.0

the bad guys... When the line-of-sponsorship is not protected absolutely the result is mistrust and decay which eats away at the very fabric of the business and causes chaos within the ranks.

There are few exceptions to the above rule. In cases where upline fails to support or fulfill promises or generally accepted business practices. Where abuses or corruption has infected the relationships the only appropriate and fair disposition may be a well thought out change of sponsorship.

This concept coincides with the general attitude of the society today, the "What's In It for me" generation. I take care of me and you take care of you. When you put your own downline ahead of "The Group" as a whole, destructive things can begin to happen. Remember that you are a business of one. You are an independent distributor just as each of your downline is also an independent distributor but independent of whom? The very answer to the question spawns potential disunity and suggests "fractured links" rather than a "cohesive network."

The term "Network marketing" implies people who are linked or connected together, people searching for individual financial freedom bonded together with others on the same search. If each of us embraced the concept, MY group comes ahead of THE group, then there's NO group, because under that philosophy, there are no groups, only individuals the business then is made up of a group of mavericks out to enrich themselves at the expense of others. Not a pretty picture and certainly the critics of NWM love to point out how this is more often true than not.

The beauty of network marketing is the opportunity to take advantage of the different talents in The Group, so they can help each other. Can you see the wisdom of the group concept? My upline called it "the glue." The benefits of a "The Group" philosophy:

1. Broadens our relationship base.
2. Creates a sense of security and stability
3. Varied talents and skills become available to everyone equally according to their willingness to participate.

If you promote "The group over My group" when you're not there to work it, your business can go on. If you promote your group over the rest, you've got to be there to work it all the time. Promote the spirit and general success of the entire organization so it's there to support you. This is what we rely on to provide for perpetuity in our businesses.

Securing your business requires both upline and downline help. You are the bond or link between your downline and your upline.

Events

Where so many go wrong with the concept of The Group vs. My Group is in the area of events. Not only should you concern yourself with the relationships you build with your upline and downline but your cross-line as well. (Cross-line groups are any groups that are not in your upline or downline)

Bob Crisp - Raising a Giant 2.0

You should consider not only the benefits of staying plugged in but also the damage that being unplugged can do. Let me give you an example which occurs frequently. Let's say you've got a prospect you just can't get to the weekly hotel event held on Thursday nights. You take the position, "I'm going to go see him Thursday instead of going to the group event." Big mistake! You're teaching him the wrong thing. You're teaching him that on Thursday night he doesn't need to be at The Group business opportunity event. Is it all that important? You bet it is! It's about priorities and solid business building principles. It is the very fabric on which your business relies! Teach them to build it right when they're new, and they'll never depart from it.

Internet Note: Today it might be a webinar or podcast instead of a hotel event... learn how the internet tools can help you leverage your time.

You should schedule him for another time or better yet, go get him and take him to the hotel event. Teach him one of the most important lessons you can teach him before he/she gets into business, and that is "The group" is more important than any of us individually. Adopt the philosophy that "I'm going to be in support of the organization every time the organization meets in my area." Very important. If you take that position, then every person that you sponsor, will see you in the correct role supporting The Group and the result will be that they will support you too!

You say Bob; did you always practice what you preach? Absolutely not! I paid dearly for my thoughtlessness in the end. I made all the mistakes, but this one was the biggest one. In the phenomenal growth spiral of my early years in network marketing I stayed aligned and plugged in. However, as my group grew so did my ego and I forgot the things that got me there. I let MY group take precedence over THE group and began to cut my people off from a source of power that they needed to continue successfully.

At the point I pulled the plug on my upline I unknowingly cut myself off from a vital link to the power and performance of some pretty talented performers. These were people I needed but didn't know I needed. I set myself up for a pull out by my own more successful downline who when they got into trouble went wisely back to my (and their) upline to get "plugged in" again.

Lesson:

Always stayed plugged in to the original source of "The System" put any "The Group" function, web-based seminar or event ahead of your own personal success… in the end it will mean everything to you

De-edification is a killer and it takes many forms! A raised eyebrow or a snide comment, a put down or outright negative remark about someone can destroy a significant portion of your credibility and future business.

Having been through the entire cycle of ups and downs in the business several times, I can honestly tell you that this is the area where no mistakes are left unnoticed.

Bob Crisp - Raising a Giant 2.0

I used what I believed to be good judgment, but my frame of reference was in another industry. In the life insurance business everything was so well defined and organized. Everything seemed to me to be so disorganized with my network marketing upline. I wanted to "normalize" the network marketing industry. Of course I wanted to use my definition of "normal."

I just couldn't understand why so many things were done at odd hours. They would call events at eleven or twelve o'clock at night sometimes several hundred miles away. Reluctantly, I would go with my leaders in tow.

I would have an opportunity event early in the evening in Tulsa and my leaders and I would drive to some distant spot like Dallas, which is about 200 miles or so away for a late night or early morning leadership and planning event. (Incidentally, we never judged how far something was by the number of miles. We judged by the number of (tapes) CDs it took to get there. Tulsa, Oklahoma to Dallas, Texas is only four CDs away!)

Internet Update: Today we may use Ipods or MP3 players or plug CDs into our car's sound systems.

Looking back today the times that I spent on the road with my upline and downline associates were some of the greatest times of building and bonding that we ever had in our lives. Those late night drives when we drove hundreds of miles for a event and then turned around at two o'clock in the morning and drive those same miles back arriving home just before dawn so that we could shower and change and then go to work the next day without ever having an ounce of

BOB CRISP - RAISING A GIANT 2.0

sleep were very special times. A small piece perhaps to the puzzle but a very important one.

Why, you might ask, would we put ourselves through those experiences? I guess we knew it could mean financial freedom for us and we were willing to pay whatever price it took for that freedom!

I remember hearing someone say "Success is built on Inconvenience." I made the decision to do whatever it takes. Another piece of the puzzle... Commitment. Have you noticed how some people are just willing to let life pass them by? They're "saving themselves" for some great moment in time when they are going to "give it all." The problem is, that day never comes and they die having never done anything with all their might. They miss out on this piece of the puzzle and wonder later why?

There are people out there who won't do what you will do. That's what makes you a "three-percenter" and not a member of the larger club of compromisers who won't do what is required for success and then wonder why their lives are so mundane and incomplete. Remember the lesson of the most important part... The Missing pieces!

How can you work with someone who is not committed? Why not take time to discover the stumbling blocks to commitment? Find the missing pieces then go on!

Today, I live on the west coast in Wells Fargo Country. They have an advertisement for Wells Fargo Bank that pictures a bunch of riders on galloping horses. The caption says...

Bob Crisp - Raising a Giant 2.0

"You either make dust, or eat dust."

I determined I was going to be one of those people making dust. How about you? "The System" promotes unity and showcases new habit patterns. These new habit patterns provide the climate and stimulus for growth. As you build with your organization, you'll find the people that will develop habits that they learned from seeing others perform at levels higher than their own.

How fast is fast?

You don't know whether you're fast until you run against someone who is faster. Habit patterns determine the reaction time of your leaders, which in turn promotes growth or stagnation.

How can you tell when somebody's not plugged in to The Group"? Quite simply, they're out of sync with the rest of the group. They don't come to events except when they have a prospect or when they are speaking. They don't use the same teaching materials. They speak negatively of others in the group and create dissension in the organization. They run down the company, the product, the upline, or the marketing program.

Those that are unplugged tend to innovate instead of duplicate. They are on the "idea of the month program." These people confuse the new distributors. Once an established pattern is created, it is important if not imperative to stick to it. You can't keep changing the pattern or the system. If you keep changing it all the time, no one knows what's happening. When everybody does the business differently, nobody knows how to do it.

Am I against innovative ideas? No. On the contrary I believe the best ideas for building are ahead not behind. However, there are some things that have proven to work in the past over and over again. Learn the business first then make changes only when you have considered all the possible consequences. The old adage "if it ain't broke don't fix it" applies. Focus on stability and continuity.

The 1980 United States Olympic hockey team won the Gold Medal at Lake Placid. They did so by beating the mighty Russian hockey juggernaut. The Russians, unlike the Americans, were professionals in every sense of the definition. They played hockey and got paid for it.

The U.S. hockey team, however, was made up of second rate college players who played for a country where ice hockey rated somewhere behind chicken plucking as a spectator sport.

Herb Brooks was the team's coach, himself not a stellar performer. Sports Illustrated said "Herb Brooks molded that group of 'also-rans' into a team so that the whole became greater than the sum of its parts." The victory helped give a nation, who had just come out of a nasty war in Vietnam, back its pride.

A hockey team did what a President or Congress could not do. People celebrated for weeks! America the beautiful, long may she live! Pride… Confidence… Peace. All parts of the puzzle.

Bob Crisp - Raising a Giant 2.0

The system pulls the group together so that the sum becomes greater than the individual parts. Everyone not just the strong, talented, and good looking can win too! We're a team! Just as the hockey team pulled a nation back together, so can victories by other members of the team you are on. Pull your team together. When "The group" is larger there's always someone getting a bite out of the apple of success. Celebrate the victories and pull your team together. It gives us all hope!

Does it work? Can you go from 100 to 10,000 people in 90 to 120 days? Is it possible? I was recently with a company that went from zero distributors to 40,000 in their first year of operations. Of the 40,000 only 3,000 were actually active. In the next twelve months we went to over 200,000 distributors! Talk about exponential growth!

How did we do it? Simple. We used "The System That Never Fails". If a company can start-up and in a year have 40,000 distributors, then you, by using this same system, can have 40,000 distributors a year from now. Why not? If anyone can do it, then why can't you do it? The answer is simple. You can do it if there's a vehicle, if there's a system in place, and if you understand how to drive the vehicle. It's the difference between going out this week and sponsoring three new people and next week all four of you going out and sponsoring three each rather than you going it alone.

The story of most in network marketing is that they don't get others involved in the system early enough to do any good. The average new distributor quits before he or she is ever plugged in. Don't let this happen to you. When

BOB CRISP - RAISING A GIANT 2.0

you sign someone up the first thing to do is to begin building a bond between them and your upline. Get them plugged in!

I attended the Indianapolis 500 for several years. It is a spectacular event as anyone who's ever been can attest. At the end of the race the winning car pulls into victory lane and enters "The Winners Circle." A pretty girl comes out and congratulates the winner. She kisses the driver not the car!

The driver couldn't have won without the vehicle but the driver gets the winners check and the kiss. In network marketing you must have a vehicle designed to win! It is essential to have a pit crew that knows how to fix the vehicle when it's broken or make adjustments when it's not performing at its best.

When you have the right system you can worry about driving the car. When you have to worry about the vehicle (system) you are diverted from driving. Incidentally, you may have to learn how to drive the vehicle. It may take some time and certainly a couple of times around the track will not make you a professional driver but stick with the program. Perfect practice makes perfect.

Try the "System That Never Fails." Join a winning team and drive for victory lane! Go back to the beginning of this chapter and review the key elements of "The System." Make sure you and your group is looking out for each other. Emphasize how important each person is to the outcome. Stay plugged in to your upline! Follow the person who is following a worthwhile dream. Be a part of something bigger than you. Take pride in yourself, your company, your upline, and your products.

Duplicate don't innovate. Practice what you preach. Use a uniform program for training and recognition. "The system" will stand up to the test of time and secure the future for you and yours.

Chapter Five

The Art vs. The Science

"Nothing splendid has ever been achieved except by those who dared believe that something inside them was superior to the circumstances."
--- Bruce Barton

Like many of you, I have for years been awed by the price of old paintings. Probably the most valuable and most well known painting in the world hangs in the Louvre in Paris...Leonardo Da Vinci's "Mona Lisa." On my first trip to Paris a few years ago my traveling companions and I decided that we should see the Louvre as well as the Eiffel Tower, Notre Dame Cathedral and the other well known Paris landmarks in a grand stretch of about 36 hours. Power Tourism for sure!

We made the Louvre our second stop with the express purpose of seeing the Mona Lisa. Because vandals had damaged the painting the previous year, the curator of the museum had placed a bullet proof glass over the painting. A crowd of 80-100 milled around the greatest painting in the world. As I stood there and examined this magnificent work of art, I was at a loss as to why the painting was so valuable.

Bob Crisp - Raising a Giant 2.0

It wasn't the beauty of the lady in the painting. I thought we have girls back in America that are much prettier. Certainly she was no fashion statement. The reason for my confusion was simple. I didn't have the training to be able to appreciate the subtle hues and tones or masterful brushwork or the way Da Vinci captured her beguiling smile. In short, I was looking at the wrong elements of the painting.

Network marketing is an art as well as a science. It is not our intent here to establish the science in detail but to explore the art form. To appreciate the masterful way people who know this art build great businesses, takes years of training. What must be learned to build a large successful network marketing organization is the difference between the art and the science.

The "Science" of the business is the technique of building depth, memorizing sales tracks and business presentations. Knowing how to use your internet driven "Back Office."

Internet Note: emarketing is today's version of the "CDs that worked" When done correctly it can provide you with so many of the benefits previous systems lacked. Find out from your upline or company what system they use for emarketing solutions and if they don't exist try www.allaxismedia.com

Making the bonus plan work for you. Necessary things to know and use! But it is not how well you memorize sales tracks that count; it is how well you deliver the sales track that puts the bacon on the table. (Make use of online videos and dynamic internet tools to shortcut the road to success) Michelangelo could have painted houses but he would have been an unknown painter not a world famous artist.

Anyone can learn and teach the science of the business. It may take years before you begin to learn the difference between doing and teaching, between activity and accomplishment, between innovation and duplication, emulation and imitation. Study with the masters and become a master!

I know many people who can sponsor, and teach the science with great proficiency, but cannot seem to put together a cohesive unit or organization with staying power. They lose bodies as fast as they can sponsor them and inevitably find themselves at odds with emerging leaders within their own downline group.

The basic ability that most of us possess to deal with people at the entry level is inadequate to deal with leaders who are growing in income and changing their self-image. Egos become inflated, feelings get hurt, and the simple "little" business we started with gets very complex and stressful.

To deal with this growing phenomenon we must learn the art form of the business. This study takes a good deal of time and experience. Confidence and power come only with experience. I can show you what to look for, how to sharpen your eye and to hone your skills, but to be a leader in network marketing you must lead. The word leader is a verb not a noun.

Bob Crisp - Raising a Giant 2.0

Vince Lombardi, the deceased fabled coach of the Green Bay Packers said, "The new leadership is in sacrifice, it is in self-denial. It is in love, it is in fearlessness. It is in humility and it is in perfectly disciplined will. This is also the distinction between great and little men."

Leadership is an art form. The "style" in which we perform our tasks as leaders becomes as important as the substance of our tasks. Just as it takes time to learn to paint or sing at a professional level, so it takes time to learn the nuances of the network marketing industry.

Dealing with our own egos as we learn is perhaps the hardest job of all. We have a tendency to take the stance that since we were good enough to get where we are, we must be good enough to go on. The fact is, that what got you here won't take
you there. Personal growth is essential. It is a desirable part of living.

The art form of network marketing lies mostly in how we deal with the stresses and strains of a dynamically growing business. Notice the way people change as they begin to gain in confidence. They take on interesting new traits. They will even walk differently. Their attitudes change and they notice what you do more.

The Dale Carnegie people spend hours teaching their students to shake hands and smile, to look others in the eye when talking to them. The skills developed in communication aren't learned in a classroom but honed on the streets and in the living rooms and dens of new distributors.

BOB CRISP - RAISING A GIANT 2.0

Maxwell Maltz in his book "Psycho-Cybernetics" tells of the positive changes which occurred in many of his patients after surgery but marveled at the lack of change in others. It amazed and confused him that he could perform the same basic surgery on two different patients and one would look in the mirror and see a beautiful new face while the other whose physical results were equally beautiful, would look in the mirror and see the same scarred and ugly creature that she was before the surgery. It was then that he began to realize the importance of self-image.

They said of Lombardi that he seemed to know who to pat on the back and who to kick in the backside. A reporter asked him one day how he learned to do this so well. He replied, "I kicked the ones I should have patted and patted the ones I should have kicked until I learned to tell the difference." His skills with his players came from years of doing it wrong. When working with people you can throw the sciences out the window, for as certain as God made little green apples people will surprise you.

The National Football League has an interesting system for keeping the balance of power in the league. They allow the worst teams from the previous year to draft the best college players for their team. This should mean that the worst teams become the best and that the best teams become the league doormats. The fact is that the best teams seem to always be at the top.

The reason is that winning teams seem to get more out of their players. Most agree this is art. The science of blocking and tackling, passing and running are the same, but in a league made up of teams stocked with All Americans the ones who remain at the top are the ones who apply the art form better than the rest.

Study the way someone you admire speaks or smiles or shakes hands and the way they treat people. Study the way they apply the laws of prosperity. You'll soon notice that they have ways of attracting quality distributors as well as getting more out of distributors who would normally be considered average at best. They have a knack of moving people along to the next level. Their products are the same as yours. They get the same bonuses (only theirs is bigger). They just seem to have it.

Luck? To be sure some people seem to be luckier than others, but this happens far too often to ascribe the continued success of others to mere luck. Learn the art form and you will be luckier too!

Just as fundamentals such as blocking and tackling are important in football, so are the basics of network marketing important in the continued success of your organization. The science consists of contacting and inviting, retailing the product, teaching, speaking with clarity, follow-up and follow-through techniques, and staging events, online webinars and podcasts and live events.

There have been hundreds of books written about these subjects and they will each bring you some added skill and information that you will find helpful.

Here we want to focus primarily on the study of the art form, leadership development and the dynamics of groups and organizations. Don't leave out the science however; it is the element of study that you must not miss.

Bob Crisp - Raising a Giant 2.0

The principle of art in network marketing is simple. Multiply your efforts by teaching others to do what you do. For the effort you will receive a handsome reward. Why then do so many people miss the mark?

A look at modern business would reveal that most people going into business for themselves are not skilled entrepreneurs as one would believe, but technicians with good ideas but little sense of what is going to be required to turn them into successful business ventures.

Today, anyone wishing to be in business for themselves is looking at a six figure investment and eighty to ninety hour work weeks to accomplish any degree of success.

The entrepreneur of today must be good at marketing and sales, accounting and inventory control, as well as being well versed in data processing, management and possibly manufacturing.

The network marketing industry provides would-be entrepreneurs with a training ground for success, a place where you can explore the areas you are weakest in and get help from someone who's been there before.

A good network marketing company has training and business development programs which are staged or incremented to allow you to grow at your own pace. Cookie-cutter growth programs rarely work since we are all coming to the business with varying degrees of experience. Society has taught us to look in the wrong places for the answers. Many stumble around for years gathering knowledge and forgetting wisdom. I call these people the "educated

BOB CRISP - RAISING A GIANT 2.0

ignorant." The great un-washed who worship at the altar of information but miss the entire point of life... that we are looking for results not mere information.

In the Broadway show "Dreamgirls" a soul singer named Jimmy sees his career going on the rocks. He storms off stage after one of his miserable performances and shouts at his manager and girl friend "These songs don't work anymore!" The manager replies, "That's because Jimmy, you don't trust the words and Jimmy you don't trust the music."

Like Jimmy, so many of us go through life crucifying our careers and destroying our opportunities because we haven't learned to trust the music. We have grown deaf to the harmonies of life and have allowed ourselves to wonder aimlessly about.

In your quest for network marketing success you will be confronted daily with people who suffer from lack of trust. They will look to you to tell them what to do to be successful then freeze up with fear because they don't trust you or the information (music?). The temptation is to give them the same old tired song and dance of "See the people and sell the products," but if that was the cure they would have cured themselves. They already know they need to see more people. And as for selling more products? They don't have to be told twice that the key to making money is selling products.

So what's the answer? And where do you learn to handle these not so easy to answer questions? The answer is leadership. Working with people is pure art. Being a leader means dealing with people who are not focused or

BOB CRISP - RAISING A GIANT 2.0

committed to their own goals or objectives. It's up to you to steer them in the right direction or keep them in long enough for someone else to turn them around.

Early in someone's business experience you should look to form a bond of trust that will lead the way for them to make a commitment to their business success. Try to get them to understand your sincere desire for their success and that the only philosophy that will work for you both is a "win/win" philosophy. This philosophy hopefully will lead the new distributor to a point of making a long-term commitment to go beyond the pain to find the gain.

Early in the game let them know that success won't come easy but it will be worth the price they may have to pay. This coincides with the practice of telling the customer less and giving those more rather than delivering less than you promised. Unreasonable expectations can produce devastating disappointment.

Kathy Miller was a young girl of about fourteen when she crossed Scottsdale Road in front of a car doing fifty miles an hour. The crunch of her young body against the front of the car could be heard a mile away. When the ambulance arrived, they pronounced her dead on the scene. Then her hand moved slightly and the paramedic found a faint pulse.

She was transferred to a hospital and put into intensive care. She lay in a coma for several weeks. Her weight dropped to just over seventy pounds! The doctors told her family not to expect her to ever come out of the coma. Her mother Barbara refused to give up hope. She bathed her, combed her hair, told her how beautiful she was, and prayed for her constantly.

Then one day Kathy awakened. Like some sleeping angel she opened her eyes. She couldn't talk, walk or even feed herself, but she was alive! Her parents took her home, fed her, bathed her and carried her like a baby. Slowly, Kathy began to recover. They taught her to eat with a fork, to walk with a walker but still she was discouraged, depressed and listless.

Kathy's mother said to her one day, "Kathy you've got to stop counting the empties, you've got to start counting the blessings. Kathy Miller you need a goal." "What do you want to do more than anything in the world?" Kathy Miller, who had been a runner before the accident, said "I want to run again." Run? Why, she could hardly walk! But Kathy's mother said, "OK, run it is." It took a while, but Kathy Miller, who only months before was pronounced dead on a Scottsdale, Arizona street, ran in the Phoenix marathon! Oh, you won't find her name among the first finishers. No, as a matter of fact, if you were there watching the race you would have been the last to leave except for the Miller family.

Some fourteen hours after the starter's gun had sounded Kathy came trotting, slowly dragging one foot into the stadium, sweat pouring from her body, and agony on her face. "Alright," her father yelled at her still a mile from the finish, "You've made your point! Stop! Give it up! Everyone else has gone home. It's just you, let's go home." But little Kathy Miller was having nothing to do with quitting. She simply brushed her father aside and continued her quest. She said, "I may not win but I'm going to finish!"

BOB CRISP - RAISING A GIANT 2.0

What makes a winner? Is there such a thing as a "born winner"? I don't think so. I think Kathy Miller was a product of parents who wouldn't give up on her. She was a result of doctors and nurses who wouldn't quit attending to her most personal and private needs. I have little patience or sympathy for quitters but am long-suffering and patient with those who get up every morning looking to slay the dragons in their lives! These are the true G I A N T S!

I believe that winning is a learned thing. So is losing! I believe that losers can become winners and that winning is an art form taught by winners. Study winners. Study their habits, their speech, what they wear, how they stand and walk. Find out what they read, who they listen to and catch the essence of their souls.

A bystander asked the sculptor, "How do you make a horse out of a block of granite?" The sculptor replied, "You simply chip away everything that doesn't look like a horse!"

Art or science? Emotion or logic? Products or people? Here's the success formula Art + Emotion x People = Healthy, happy, successful business experience.

Lesson: It's always too soon to quit. Hang with winners and become like them

Chapter Six

The Duplication Principle

"I would rather have one percent of a hundred men's efforts than one hundred percent of my own." -- J. Paul Getty.

Leveraging our time and energy through others is the vital missing link for most of us. Those who are willing to settle for a job, who finds the uncertainty of being in business for themselves unsettling will never find financial independence. "The crowd" usually goes for the security instead of the opportunity.

Oprah Winfrey, the talk show host, earned over 90 million dollars last year as a "syndicated" performer. Compare that to David Letterman's mere 14 million dollars at CBS. Letterman has a job, Winfrey owns her own show. Granted most of us would be content with the 14 mil. But where does the other 80 million dollars go? Into the pocket of the network. Certainly Letterman's value approximates Winfrey's. The difference is who takes the risk. Letterman transfers the risk to the network, Oprah takes the risk herself.

Note: Letterman since this was originally written formed a company called "Worldwide Pants" and not only owns his own show but many others. Smart people eventually "get it"

BOB CRISP - RAISING A GIANT 2.0

usually from someone like Oprah who was an early investor with Nike too.

In dollars and years comparison then, Oprah spends one year earning what it takes David Letterman six years to earn. Not only is Oprah making more money but she is also leveraging her time. It takes most people forty years to earn a million dollars and when they do they usually discover they are still broke… Old and broke. Not a pretty picture.

Network marketing offers us the chance to learn the skills while we minimize the risks involved. Through the principle of duplication we enter a mentorship program and get to take our time in the process. The decision of fast or slow is ours. I prefer fast. Maybe you prefer to take your time. In any case we can bite off as much as we want to chew at any given time.

Through the duplication process you have a simple but effective way of learning skills while earning an income with little or no capital at risk! Through this same process you can learn to emulate rather than imitate success. Your mentors have a direct financial incentive to help and teach you to succeed. No one benefits by your demise. Your upline plays an essential role in your development process.

When I first looked at the industry I asked my sponsor how the products were sold. He said, "Each one sells a little bit." I figured if each one only sold a "little bit" it would take a lot of people to sell a lot. I was right. It does take a lot of people. What I could not imagine however was how easy it was going to be over all to find a lot of people. I only had to find a handful. It was the duplication process that made it possible.

Try making a list of the things your sponsor does. Now work your way upline toward the most successful person you know. Ask yourself how you stack up to them. If you are just evaluating your chances in network marketing, visualize what the elements are that you would need to be successful.

How many of the key elements do you have? Where are your weaknesses? How will you acquire the skills needed to advance? What will you do to gain the knowledge and skills your group will need to see in you for you to rise to the top?

There is a mistaken belief among some today that network marketing is simply a matter of sponsoring some distributors, loading them up with products, and then telling them to go sell them. It's no wonder so many fail. The training and personal development programs of most companies fall miserably short. They leave us wondering how to get people involved in programs which are designed only to perpetuate a myth and not designed to get at the real issues of personal growth and true business success!

MY upline admonished me that "personal growth preceded business growth."

We get duplication alright, but duplication of all of the wrong things. We are told to do what our upline or sponsor did and so we do it without thinking much about the ramifications down the road. Or, because we are unskilled in some of these areas, we simply fade into the sunset with an epitaph written over our graves "Here lies another failed believer."

Bob Crisp - Raising a Giant 2.0

Internet Note:

Today, thanks to the internet, everyone has access to the learning resources required to develop our skills in business. Perhaps the best source is my company's website www.allaxismedia.com.

Perhaps we would have done better, responded more positively and enthusiastically, if we had some serious training and an organization or system to work in and develop before being sent out to die in the streets without so much as an hour of field training.

To be fair it is the business itself which sometimes perpetuates this error by growth so fast that training everyone one-on-one is impossible. The nature of fast growth is such that years can go by and by all appearances the business is hugely successful but an essential building block is missing in the foundation which can cause the building to crumble and fall eventually. The blame for such failure is never placed where it belongs but is usually laid at the feet of poor management or inadequate funding or government interference.

What parents do in moderation… children do in excess.

Duplication is a fact of life. Children emulate what their parents, teachers and role models do…in spite of what former NBA star Charles Barkley says… he and all the other well-known athletes are "role models." We are serving today as examples or symbols for someone, our children, our friends, our neighbors and associates. Are we doing well?

Are we proud of the example we are setting? Will we be happy to see our "business children" grow up to be like we are? If this is beginning to sound like a lecture on parenthood, well maybe it is. From one leader to another, watch what you do, someone is following your example.

Relatability

Being relatable is the single most important issue facing network marketers. You will find that the broader one's experience the more relatable he or she is. As an example, if you are a football nut but never watched ice hockey you probably wouldn't know what the term "Icing the puck" meant. Your ability to relate to a hockey nut would be restricted to other areas of mutual interest.

The first axiom of duplication is "Your group will do what you do." That's the safe bet, only like children they tend to copy mostly the bad habits and ignore the good ones. If they see you with a stack of training CDs in the front seat of your car, before you know it, the leaders in your organization will have a stack of CDs (usually smaller than yours) in the front seat of their car.   If they see you wear nice clothes to events, they'll do likewise. (A bit of a note here is appropriate. "Nice" does not have to mean expensive. Sometimes the more expensive you dress the more intimidating you can be. Don't overdress.)

Relatability is finding a common ground from which to build new relationships. While this may seem simple, and sometimes it is, it is vital that you and your new group acknowledge that "business" relationships are based on your ability to relate on many levels. People who relate only on one level usually find network marketing a difficult and frustrating journey.

Years ago I learned to relate the issue of relatability to a funnel. The dictionary describes a funnel as -" a tube with a cone-like mouth, for pouring things into containers with a small mouth."

For our purposes this funnel represents the concept of borrowing influence from the people around you while expanding your own level of influence. While it is impossible to relate to everyone it is possible to expand our level of relatability.

Just as a funnel has a broad cone-like flange, our personal funnel has a flange of relatability depicting the broader base of experience that some have over others. People who have lived in restricted environments all their lives have narrower levels of experience. Those who go to a college in another state, enlist in the armed forces, travel, and study or research widely tend to have a broader level of experience.

Bob Crisp - Raising a Giant 2.0

With our organizational funnel the consequences of a narrow base of relatability is lessened. You can take advantage of the funnel consisting of your key upline and cross-line team members by introducing your prospects to people of comparable background. In this way you are borrowing influence or credibility from those around you and are more apt to succeed in the sponsoring process than if you rely solely on your own level of experience.

It is precisely for this reason that "the system" is so vital. Those who succeed in network marketing inevitably learn how to make the most of this "influence alliance."

Broadening your level of relatability is time consuming but simple… Read a broad sampling of books, attend as many events and meet as many new people as possible. Let your natural curiosity get involved. Ask questions of those you meet such as "What caused you to get involved in this business?" And "what is the key to your success?" Don't be afraid to ask a stupid question. Take time to find out the background stories of those around you. Find a mentor. Chances are it will be someone in your upline whose success and style you admire and would like to emulate.

Try associating with people who are NOT like you. What can you learn from those whose experience is similar to your own that will help you? You may get your ego stroked or your own ideas reinforced but you probably won't grow.

The key to new levels of relatability is exploring new levels of awareness. This goes against our basic tendencies and therefore is a concept which takes some getting used to.

BOB CRISP - RAISING A GIANT 2.0

Your challenge then is not only to get yourself to stretch and grow but to lead your new recruits into an expanded awareness of their need to grow. What can you do to facilitate this growth process?

Try sharing a new book with them. Don't just give them a book but tell them something interesting that you learned from the book. Read them a passage and point out that you felt they would enjoy it too. Take them to a seminar in your area. Attend a local networking group. Better yet start a networking group of your own. Analyze these steps to achieving a broader base of relatability.

1. Communications
2. **Public Relations**
3. Sales
4. Teaching
5. Leadership

Duplication requires a thorough knowledge of the job to be done. How can you duplicate that which you have no knowledge or awareness of? In each of the steps listed above the education process can take years to master. Determine today to take the beginning steps that will lead you to be better at each of the skills.

The duplication process displays itself most in our attitudes toward personal growth. Demonstrating an open spirit and inquisitive mind will encourage your distributors to be open to you. Have a "can do" attitude. Get a sense of urgency about what you are doing. People love to follow people who know where they are going and are on their way.

The greater your sense of urgency the higher your groups sense of urgency. Develop a do it now attitude and message. Don't procrastinate or put off doing things.

Two seagulls were flying around over an airport one day when a fighter plane took off and narrowly missed them. Once they had recovered from the shock, one bird looked at the other and said, "I bet you wish you could fly like that!" The other replied, "I could if my tail was on fire."

Lesson:

Get on fire and people will come from miles around just to watch you burn! Give your distributors something to shoot for. Know that if they are duplicating you they are duplicating the best!

Chapter Seven

Who Shall Be The Greatest?

"You will become as small as your controlling desire, or as great as your dominant aspiration." -- James Allen

In organizations of all kinds there is a constant struggle for position or power. Over time centers of power change and regimes fall and are replaced by different regimes. Businesses, civic groups, universities, and of course governments go through constant power struggles and leadership changes. Network marketing is no different, only here the power ultimately accrues to performance over politics.

A network marketing company is like a big long chain. While a chain is a series of circles, squares or rectangles interlocked to form a continuous string of links, a network marketing company is a series of people linked together by a "line-of-sponsorship" to form a long line or chain.

As in every growing organization the question soon arises as to who is the most important person in the chain? What are the criteria on which to fairly judge who and what is important in a network marketing chain? Is it who got in first? How about the one who makes the most money? Or the one who is the best trainer? Maybe it is the one who can motivate best or provide the best all around guidance and leadership.

The First Link Theory

Many could make the argument that the first link, the one connected directly to the company is the most important. Certainly in most modern day network marketing companies the person at the top is the one who makes the most money, so it would stand to reason that the first people to get in and pay the price of new beginnings would be the greatest. The problem with assigning greatness to the first link is that quite often the first link is merely an extension of the founder's family or friends who had lots of faith but little if anything to do with the building of the business.

The subsequent links could also claim greatness for each can argue, (accurately I might submit) that they too are deserving of credit for being the greatest. Without one link the chain ceases to be. Each link then shares a distinctly different value and yet an equally distinct importance.

The last or most recent link in the chain could always argue for greatness because the last link represents the future. The ability for any network marketing company to grow always lies in the last links. The "leading edge" of the business defines the future and makes the ongoing viability of the company possible.

So what is the answer to the question who is the greatest? In the pages that follow we will look at some important ways to evaluate and judge the "chain" or line-of-sponsorship.

The Income Theory

The first item on the agenda for discussing value is income. Many considerations must be evaluated. First, does each member of the chain make money in the same way? In other words, does any member have a better or more lucrative deal? If so, re-figure the income figures on the same basis for a fair look at the numbers. Numbers don't lie, but they also don't tell the whole story either.

For example, newer distributor groups will usually do substantially higher sales volume per distributor than a more seasoned one will because of initial start up inventory. However, inventory purchases can come back. Distributors get disenchanted and return products, so upline commissions can reflect an inventory loading scheme which ultimately backfires on the company and costs the company large sums, not to mention considerable credibility problems in the community at large and in the industry.

Income, while the major reason most people get involved with network marketing, it is a secondary judgment factor because many of the "levels based" bonus programs allow you to make considerable income from having recruited only one real "hitter." Break-away volume based plans on the other hand are more difficult for the average distributor to make money but they certainly cut the men from the boys when it comes to evaluating who is actually building the business.

The discussion then comes down to the fact that the only constant way to judge distributor effort and ability is a combination of width, (number of legs across your front line) and depth, (number of distributors downline in any particular leg). Width generally indicates that you, not your upline or downline, are out on the sponsoring trail and event new customers and prospective distributors. While upline players may help you sponsor width, it usually is in their best interest to concentrate on working in the depth of your organization.

Working depth can produce large amounts of volume and sometimes, depending on the pay plan, can produce significant incomes, but it is often a dodge for going out and using your own skills and prospect lists to develop the business. Sometimes distributors retreat to working depth so that someone else will have to make the phone calls and set up the events and they won't have to.

Obviously, someone who builds only one large leg is not as proven a success as someone who has built many different legs to a high level. Therefore, the discussion of income ends when evaluating who is the most important player in the chain, with a discussion of width and depth.

Most companies have a recognition program based on the amount of sales volume, number of legs in width you have at a certain sales volume, and your own personal group sales volume. Many have retail sales requirements which must be met in order to receive bonuses and recognition. (I believe we will see more of this in the future)

The Training Theory

Many discussions of who is the most important revolve around the issue of training. Certainly, when you are building an organization of part-time sales people who are for the most part transitioning from another career, you will want to address the importance of being a good trainer.

Training is transference of ideas, skills and methods to another. The better you are at doing this, the more valuable you will be to your organization. Anything that increases your training skills will enhance your value and thus move you along the chain more quickly.

This certainly is born out in society as a whole. A college education, together with on the job or specialized training, is the launching platform for advancement in almost any company. Entrepreneurs usually get lost somewhere along the way and must look outside of themselves to someone more experienced in a given area to teach them and strengthen their skills.

In a network marketing organization you may find that a great downline will emerge with both width and depth, but the key player in the training area may come from the company, from an upline leader or from someone in another organization. What any of these scenarios may be telling us is that we have a smart recruiter who is smart enough to get his/her distributors to another person for training, but is not skilled enough themselves to do the training. I have personal acquaintances that do quite well in network marketing but are not especially good trainers themselves.

This lack of skill may be the result of indifference, which tells us we are dealing with a weak overall player, or it may stem from a defect of some kind such as a speech impediment or poor vocabulary, or it may stem entirely from lack of experience. Regardless, no evaluation of value within the framework of a network marketing organization would be complete if we did not discuss the role of the trainer.

Training itself has many levels for it is possible that someone is a great basic trainer but is weak in advanced leadership or sales skills development.

The Motivator Theory

No network marketing organization will go far unless someone assumes the role of the motivator. While it is true that everyone is a motivator of sorts, the kind of motivation required to sustain a long term network marketing business is much different than that required to get someone to simply sign an application and sell a few products.

The motivator we are discussing here is a provocateur, a stimulator, a visionary who has great verbal skills and is highly professional in the expression of dreams and concepts. It is important to note here that many people play essential roles in motivation.

No one is motivated simply by outside influences... a large part of motivation is found within. The motivator we are discussing here is the person to whom the organization looks to initiate programs and is the leading spokesperson for the group. He may be a provocateur, dynamic forceful personality or a simplifier who articulates in understandable terms the necessary elements of successful business building. He or she is an enabler... an encouragement to all from the least to the greatest.

Motivation is an on-going problem for all of us. The person who builds a great organization knows this all too well and plans for motivational activities everyday. The motivator may not be a great speaker but may be someone who is skilled at simplifying ideas and communicating exciting ideas and plans.

Motivating is an art form. Whether by speech or by other forms of communication, the motivator is a valued and priceless commodity in any network marketing company. There are many who believe that motivation can be bought. Just pay a fee and bring in a great motivational speaker. While this kind of motivation may work on a temporary basis, it will never take the place of native talent. Some hired guns leave you "all dressed up with no place to go." Learning to apply motivation to a productive result is the key.

This may be the area where most organizations fail ultimately. The great motivators are usually driven by the need for recognition themselves. Some however, fall into the trap of focusing so much on themselves that they fail in their mission to motivate others because they are so self-absorbed.

It would be well to understand and constantly remind ourselves that every one of us has an insatiable hunger to feel important. Again here, as with the trainer, we may find a large distributor with a large downline group and big income who is not a motivator but is good at plugging their people into someone upline, cross-line or with the company who is. This is smart business and should always be the way leaders think. The real leader has a philosophy of doing things the best way not just his way.

The Knowledge Theory

No one doubts that knowledge is the key to success. The value of being knowledgeable in determining who is the most valuable cannot be underestimated. Certainly the one who knows the most is the most apt to provide all the attributes that have been discussed to this point.

Knowledge is power - rather the use of knowledge is power.

Internet Note: Paul Zane Pilzer in his book "The Next Millionaires" says the future millionaires are those who learn "Intellectual Distribution" which he describes as "teaching others about new products and services and what these new products can do for them." And of course, the new medium for "intellectual distribution" is the internet itself. Emarketing!

Many people go through life oblivious to the things around them. There are so many are in darkness that the light is almost eclipsed. There are too many among us content with the status quo, too many unwilling to examine new ideas and methods, too many contented with mediocrity and too few motivated to learn.

The power in the future will flow to those who have and use the widest variety of available knowledge. This has never been more true than it is today in network marketing. The industry is changing. The network marketing professional has emerged and legal battles rage every day on what is acceptable business practices and what is not. Methods that could be used just a few short years ago are now considered unethical and out-dated.

The day has come for the knowledgeable to come forward and lead the way. It will always be true that while it may not take a genius to build the business, it will take someone willing to learn that which he or she does not know, to build a large, successful and long term network marketing business. Certainly the use of knowledge is very powerful.

The Leadership Theory

No one has ever become a great network marketing distributor who didn't possess great leadership skills. A leader is "One who leads the way!" Nothing can take the place of a person who gets out front and shows the way to the top. It would be an over simplification to say that setting the right example is the role of the leader. It is so much more. Leadership is an art best taught by example and learned by observation. The good leader is out front with a banner not behind with a whip.

There is, in my opinion, no higher calling on the planet than the role of the leader. Where then do you get leadership skills? Who teaches the leader to lead? How do you develop great leaders?

Leadership skills are developed over a long period of time. The true leader of any network marketing organization is never hard to find. The leader will be the most visible person around, always exhorting, challenging and motivating the group around him/her. Many times the leader is not the best trainer or most skilled speaker. Sometimes the leader is the one with the softest personality and the kindest heart. Sometimes the leader is hard-hitting and pompous, sometimes soft-spoken and humble, but always the good leader cares deeply for those he/she leads.

A good leader provides constant vision for the group. He/she provides organized events and trainings as well as reward and recognition programs for the group. A good leader is sensitive to the group's needs and desires. A good leader listens and takes into account the opinions of others. Most of all, a good leader is a decision maker! No one makes all the right decisions. A good leader makes decisions and then makes them right!

A good leader provides a sense of continuity to the group and defines boundaries of fair play that all (including himself) must follow. The leader is the lightening rod for criticism and the whipping post for the critics. The leader's ship is a lonely ship but the good leader, for all the world, would never sell out the group for the next deal. The leader's motto is "Follow me and fear nothing!"

Conclusion

Those who run away from the responsibilities which come with the success of a large network marketing business will ultimately lose it. The most important link in the chain is the one that's missing. If the chain has a distributor with knowledge, a visionary, a great communicator, a motivator, then the income will be there. It is rare when you find a chain with only one strong link. Usually each link possesses some uniqueness. The point to be learned from this chapter is not that one link is stronger than the other, but that the evaluation standards must be broad and not narrow. Income, the "usual" standard, is not "the only" standard.

There are many smaller, subtler nuances to the evaluation process. Don't judge a chain by its first or last link, nor judge it by the person with the biggest income, loudest mouth, brightest neckties or best dresses. Rather look around, take some time and get to know the persons the chain represents.

Study results, not simply activities. The race doesn't always go to the swiftest. The Good Book reminds us that "By their fruits you shall know them." Become a fruit inspector.

Over time, knowledge and leadership skills will equate to income. Over time will come testing. Through testing will emerge the real people of value. Just as the chain maker hardens the steel by putting it in the fire, so will the network marketing chain be hardened by the fires of diligence and hard work. Don't be too quick to judge. Applaud loudly for the accomplishments of others. Listen and learn. Take advantage of every opportunity to serve. Remember the admonition,

Lesson: *Let he who would be the greatest among you be as the least." The motto here should be "Stop looking for a leader and become one."*

Chapter Eight

The Ten Laws of Leadership

"Leaders are made, they are not born. they are made by hard effort, which is the price which all of us must pay to achieve any goal that is worthwhile."   -- Vince Lombardi

Motto: "I have been tried in the fires of time and tested by the winds of change… I am a Leader!"

Leadership is the key element in the development of a dynamic network marketing culture. The role of the leader is determined by many stages in the growth of an organization. The leader must be many things. His or her role changes from moment to moment. Preparation is essential. These are the ingredients that one must consider when pursuing the role of the leader.

These are laws not suggestions.

The laws of leadership, like the laws of success themselves are irrefutable. The consummate leader will use these laws to the advantage of the whole organization. Embrace them and use them and you will prosper. Ignore them and you are doomed to the bargain basement of life.

The Ten Laws of Leadership

1. The leader must have a dream larger than those he/she leads. The greatest error of most people in network marketing is that they cannot envision the scope of the business they are in. The downline groups always look upline for visionary leadership. This manifests itself most in the fact that one of the first things new distributors want to know is how well you are doing. Messages must be conveyed by example not just by verbal communication. Big dreamers inspire others to dream. Learn to communicate by example. Be aware of the people around you.

Visionary leaders establish themselves as forward thinkers. They look at the ramifications of their actions as affecting everyone. The size of your dream affects the amount of effort you are willing to put in. Your downline wants to know that you are thinking bigger so that their financial goals will coincide with yours.

2. The leader must have an attitude superior to those He/she leads. Attitude control is a constant battle. Leaders feed themselves continuously with powerful thoughts and act in an upbeat manner at all times. When you think of it, nothing else makes much sense does it?

3. The attitude leader is the one that sees the solutions and does not focus on the problems. Positive

information is gained from reading books on personal development and listening to positive thinking CDs. Positive attitudes are contagious just as negative attitudes are.

4. Negative attitudes, however, are longer lasting and have a lingering impact on the downline. One critical statement about the company, upline, or products can destroy entire legs of an organization. Negatives are expressed in word and deed. A raised eyebrow or a thoughtless comment can be indicators that the leader is neither on guard nor acting responsibly toward the business.

5. The leader takes responsibility and is first to admit when he or she has made a mistake. There is nothing more damaging to an organization than a leader who is "always right." Leaders should always understand that they are responsible for the things that go wrong in the growth of the organization, regardless of the actual responsibility. The leader sees the danger in placing blame on others and takes it himself to be the lightening rod for criticism. Additionally, the leaders should know when to demure and allow others to absorb the blows.

6. The leader is a decision maker. Nothing is more demoralizing than indecisive leadership. Someone once said a leader is concerned with doing the right thing while a manager concerns themselves with doing things right. Not all of your decisions will be correct but it is important to make decisions, then make them right rather than making right decisions. Strive for excellence not perfection. Indecision as we

will discuss later causes a sense of instability and uncertainty in the group. Be decisive. Your decisions will get better as your experiences become more diverse.

7. The leader puts those he/she leads first. There has never been a leader worth his/her salt who doesn't think of the downline first. Unfortunately today too many network marketing professionals are selfish and egocentric. They don't realize that the long term benefits of putting others first will provide much more in the end.

   During the civil war General Ulysses S. Grant was surveying the condition of his battered troops one day when he saw one of his soldiers who had no boots. General Grant said "Soldier where are your boots?" "I have none sir," came the reply. Grant got down from his horse, took off his boots and gave them to the soldier. As he was riding off he said to the soldier, "As long as I have a pair of boots... no man in my army will go without them."

   Putting those you lead first always results in a confident more aggressive organization. The Marine Corps calls it "esprit de corps." It's called "compassionate leadership." It always works.

   The leader sets the example by being out front. The typical loser tells others how to do it and sits back and watches. Leaders say "Follow me" while losers say "Go get them boys." Network marketing is a business that requires real leaders to stand up and be counted.

Poor work habits by the leader will produce the same in the downline. As previously pointed out… "What parents do in moderation, children tend to do in excess." Set the right example. Don't dig a fox hole. Take the lead. In WW II General George Patton, sometimes known as "Blood and Guts," told his troops not to dig foxholes. His theory was that they weren't going to be there long enough. He believed foxholes were for those not planning to go forward and win the war.

Foxholes are for those that are staying where they are. Since you are determined to move on, take the lead in attitude, work habits and giving, and your group will follow.

8. The leader displays a commitment to integrity and character. Because so many hopes and dreams rest on our shoulders we are obliged to exercise maximum commitment to truthfulness and honesty. Among the key issues of character are: courtesy, manners, personal conduct, respect for others and their property, truthfulness and forthrightness. In General George MacArthur's final address to the graduating class at West Point he stressed "Duty, Honor and Country."

Among other things in society today we need more people who put integrity and honor at the top of their priority list. Pride in the outfit and confidence in the leadership will be instilled at all levels when the priority is put on doing "the right thing."

9. Excellence in all things. There is no place for shoddy and inferior performance in a great network marketing organization. You are going to be associated with the worst thing you do. Unfortunately, people associate us with the cheapest or ugliest thing we do instead of the best.

   Vince Lombardi used to declare that "Winning is the only thing." I'd like to paraphrase that to say that "A commitment to winning and excellence is the only thing." Our appearance, attitude, courtesy, common caring and total dedication to excellence marks us for success or failure. Ignore these things and you will pay the price!

10. Commitment to personal growth. Personal stagnation is the cause of decay and failure in most lives. Life is dynamic! It is not static. No one wants to be around someone who is standing still. Therefore high on everyone's priority list should be a program for personal growth. However, personal growth begins with what stage each person is in your downline… here's a look at some considerations…

    Persistence and determination. No one likes to be around quitters. It takes time to achieve genuine success. Calvin Coolidge said, "Nothing can take the place of persistence. Talent will not. Nothing is more common than unsuccessful men with talent. Genius will not. Un-rewarded genius is almost a proverb. Education will not. The world is full of educated derelicts. Persistence and determination alone are omnipotent."

Someone once said, "Leadership has not been tried and found difficult, but instead has been found difficult and left largely untried." I believe those who have a genuine desire to excel will always find a way around, over or through any problem that arises.

Persistence and determination will see you through when things are darkest. When it seems you can't or shouldn't go on, the vision of what lies at the end of the trail will drive you on. Courage is what you have when the enthusiasm or inspiration that started you on the journey is gone.

These ten laws are the backbone to any successful business, but especially the network marketing business. The culture, the system, the pattern are all reliant on not just good leadership, but eventually great leadership. Pay attention to these laws and develop your skills with people and you will be a network marketing superstar. Ignore them and you'll find yourself "doing lunch" next week with "the crowd."

The 11th Law… Change IS Inevitable Pay Attention to New Internet Technologies

Leaders are the early adaptors in life. They read and listen to the trends and "see" the future. Today that means "the internet." Social networking sites, emarketing solutions, international objectives… and automated systems.

I know many people who say that "High tech" doesn't work in true "face to face" high touch selling. I point out that most of us have sit in a movie and cried or laughed out loud. This "One way" high tech medium reached out and touched or moved us... sometimes powerfully. Using high compression video and flash technology allows anyone with a video camera, a computer, and some great software the ability to "personalize" email and web media to communicate "social and economic" issues in a very warm and "High Touch" way.

There are basically five areas of PEOPLE development you should consider while building your sustainable network. My upline admonished me to "build it once" driving home the concept of Leadership Development on pathway to a stable marketing business.

Level 1 - The Neophyte – The Newbie

This person is new to network marketing and should be treated with kid gloves no matter what their previous business experience. Not that they aren't mature as individuals, but beginners need to focus on basic steps such as building lists and getting acquainted with the ins and outs of owning their own business. Learning to be a self-starter takes time and new beginners should focus on the basics.

Level 2 - Basic Techniques

Beginning leadership training. The emphasis here should be more expansive product knowledge, how to show the marketing plan and work in depth. Learn how to read people... measure commitment... solves individual problems... also you will want to learn how to utilize some basic internet emarketing solutions... social networking.

Level 3 - Advanced Leadership Training

Working depth in depth. The focus is on personal growth and leadership skills, public speaking and psychological development.

Level 4 – Beginning Leadership Development

This is the staging ground for emerging teachers and motivators. Here the focus is on working with emerging leaders and enhancing group focus. The visionary leader has to look beyond the obvious to see the possible and the impossible. Level four is a testing ground to see if you are ready to go on to

Level 5 - Advanced Leadership Development

Level five is the ultimate place reserved for the select few who have heard the call to leadership and see the possibilities beyond the horizon. Not many reach this exalted level nor do they desire to. If you have the CALL to leadership, nothing on earth can keep you from it and if not, no power can drive you to it.

Leadership skills and working with others is a constant variable. Maybe I should leave it at that because no matter what we achieve or how high we climb in life the learning process never ends.

Napoleon Hill, the author of "Think and Grow Rich" and the grandfather of modern self esteem and personal success mentors, began in the early nineteen hundreds with thirteen laws of success and by the early fifties added five more… time and history change the paradigms of success.

These are stages and are not necessarily definitive. There are training approaches that I have found appropriate to each stage. Suffice it to say the important thing here is not to over train. The only thing worse than no training is over training.

Chapter Nine
A Giant's Heart

"The eagle that soars near the sun is not concerned how he will cross the raging stream" -- Unknown

Ground floor opportunities may be for real hearty and bold pioneers. The un-initiated and timid may be better off coming into the business long after the question of success has been resolved by those willing to pay the price of new beginnings. It takes a great deal of faith in the beginning to see the vision of success that most entrepreneurs possess.

Trust and faith are inextricably tied together and without it you will find it impossible to reassure even your best prospects that everything will be okay in the new venture. Remember, most of us are risk adverse not risk inclined.

An immigrant aboard a ship coming to the United States in the 30's said to his shipmate, "I've heard that the streets of America are paved with gold. Is that true?" The shipmate replied, "No that's not true, as a matter of fact, many of the streets in America are not paved at all, the chances are you'll be doing the paving." Pioneers are a different breed. Ground floor opportunities are fraught with uncertainty as well as potential reward.

Barbara Streisand sang "People who need people are the luckiest people in the world." Nowhere is this more true than in network marketing. It takes a big heart to be able to continue in the face of major opposition.

At the heart of every great organization is a deep sense of responsibility, responsibility to members of the organization individually and as a unit. Rich Devos in his book The Compassionate Capitalist says, " The key to all success is in helping people help themselves."

There are so many great lessons to be learned from working with others. The most important lesson is the lesson of love. To be a giant learn to love more. I don't mean the romantic sense that one thinks of love, but in the deeper sense of caring about others.

At the core of the question is the sense of compassion that one brings to the arena of business and life itself. Why are you involved in network marketing if not to enhance your life and make it better? Financial gains are tied to passionate effort and persistent performance not only by you but by a confluence of others. People who are hurting need a friend not just an instructor. And don't we all hurt from time to time?

My friend and early mentor Warren Gray used to saddle up horses and he and I would ride out to some distant hilltop and he would ask me questions about life and be kind enough to listen to my rudimentary answers. I think what he was really doing was helping me to continue my search and not to rest on my early conclusions. He loved me. There's no doubt in my mind.

The glue that bonds a "group" into an "organization" is love. The missing element in so many companies is the simple heart-felt sincerity of people who love people. My mentors have taught me a great deal about the subject and I have so much more to learn.

There are the three questions that every prospect asks in his or her mind when encountering you. These questions are about love and trust. They are not mine. They were shared with me by one of my many friends and mentors.

1. Do you care for me? What every person wants to know is... do you really care for me? Do you honestly want me to succeed? Do you care if my family prospers? Do you care if I fail? Are you really thinking of me or are you merely counting the commission dollars you will make if I buy your products? If I become a distributor will you do everything you can to help me succeed?

2. Can I trust you? Are you trying to take advantage of me? Are you going to drop me like a hot potato the first chance you get? Will you be honest with me? Can I count on you? If I go to events with my guests will you be there to help me or am I on my own? When trying to qualify for the next promotion level will you consider my circumstances above your own? Will you treat my resources with integrity and can I have confidence in your advice?

3. How will your product or service make my life better or easier? The third question is one about which most sales people focus but entirely miss the point of the question. This question may be interpreted by some as simply a "buying sign" prompting a closing comment such as "Ma'am you just can't live another day without my new-fangled widget." The notion that a sales person is there to get your money while enriching himself is the accepted norm by most consumers. The sales person who truly cares about the customer is the exception.

How do you overcome the natural skepticism that all of us possess? The answer is simple. By being honest, real and straight forward. Listen to the prospect instead of selling. Share the benefits and realize that not everyone is going to buy today. Be patient. Don't push too hard. Be sensitive to others and you will win in the long run.

Super stars in all forms of life have found the short cuts frustrating and un-rewarding over time. When you press too hard you are telling others that you don't have their best interests at heart. Empathy not sympathy is the key. Networking is a matter of connecting with others. Become a rapt listener. Master the phrase "That's interesting, tell me more."

Don't get me wrong, I'm all for being positive and excited, but be positive and excited for your prospect. Questions such as, "Can you see how this product or program can enhance your financial position?" Or, "Do you see yourself in the picture?" Or, "Is there any reason why we can't get you started today?" Or, "Do you know anyone who would like to increase their income or who is looking for a career alternative?" Show that you are truly interested in your prospects well-being.

These three key questions are fear related questions. They all have to do with the fear of loss, fear of the unknown and fear of being misused.

The network marketing industry has some very common objections which require a basic knowledge of the business to overcome. You will undoubtedly run into those who will say they don't like network marketing because it "takes advantage of or uses people." They will point out that the first ones in always make all the money and that it is only a matter of time before all the opportunity is gone. What they are saying really is, "Can I trust you?" They are expressing a basic fear instinct-the fear of being used. What they really mean is abused.

The natural instinct is to accept this criticism as having some validity. The truth is that no network marketing company has ever saturated the market! If you show empathy for the question by using the simple "Feel - Felt - Found" formula you can overcome this common objection. Simply say "I know how you feel, I felt the same way, but let me tell you what I found out." The truth is the benefits accruing to those who come along later in the program are greater than those who come earlier.

Nevertheless the key to keeping an organization in place after it has been built is activities which continue to reinforce the answers to these three basic questions. What we are asked to do everyday is to reassure and to reinforce the possibilities. The equation never ends. Someone's need for reassurance never goes away. Each person in your organization needs to be told they are appreciated. They need reassurance not just in words but in so many small ways.

Internet Note:

Most of us have not learned the dynamics of using video email to keep in touch with our teams. Consider the car salesman who carries a cell phone with internet connection and a camera. He welcomes a potential car buyer and shows him the car he is thinking of buying… the first thing he does is open the car door and ask the prospective buyer to sit behind the wheel and then he takes a photograph of the buyer behind "HIS" new car… asks if he can send the photo to the prospective buyer's email… by the time the buyer gets home he has a "Thank you for stopping by" video email WITH a digital photo of himself sitting in HIS new car.

Sounds simple... But get this… so far the auto industry is clueless about its uses… the same is true with network marketers… a simple "Hi, thanks for considering my opportunity" via video email would go a long way to assist in the "Make me feel important" world of networking… so many good things happen with video email emarketing… you collect a database of prospects, customers and distributors, you can use "automated" email marketing… your retention rate will double or triple… your own activities will be magnified and more affective…

Later we will deal with the issue of recognition. In the beginning of any new relationship, business or personal, it is vital to nourish the thirst for acknowledgment daily.

Be careful of activities that destroy the fabric of this trust and love. You can unwittingly sow the seeds of destruction in an organization by ignoring the people side of the business. The culture will fail and the system breaks down and ultimately the business is gone.

Your downline wants to know "Who are you anyway? Where are you coming from? What are your motives?" The person you encounter today is going to be asking these questions.

You better have the right answers. My advice is to be upbeat and positive. Put on the new you face. Be more polite more congenial. Smile and shake hands enthusiastically. Linger longer with the hand shake and hold eye contact a bit longer than usual. Don't move on to the next person but stay and ask a personal question about their job or family followed by this most important of questions, "Is there anything I can do to help you?"

The prospective new distributor wants you to prove to him or her that you deserve their business and their respect. Will you do what it takes to gain this confidence?

Pop psychologists have tried to convince us that there's nothing wrong with us, but I've found that what the comic strip character Pogo once said is true for the most part. He said, "We have met the enemy and he is us."

The problem with "I gotta be me" is, it tends to be like the sign on the sale table at the store which says "All sales final no exchanges or refunds." The sign usually indicates there's something wrong with the products. Let's wake up to the facts. If we expect different results we've got to do different things. The same attitude will produce the same activity which will only reproduce the same results.

The hard part of becoming a Giant is not the daily activities but the need to operate in a new environment that is highly charged with human need… needs which stem from emotion and which can only be met by emotion. Failure of the individual to perform is rooted mostly in psychological and emotional makeup and is rarely found in logic or skill.

Fears need to be addressed and dealt with on a human level. Operating out of emotion instead of logic is so foreign and uncomfortable for most of us that we run to the nearest fact book and try solutions which are ill suited to the problems we face. Try a little kindness and you too will discover that the joy of seeing others succeed exceeds anything you've ever experienced. The result will be that your own goals will become reality.

Make up your mind today that your appearance, personality, and manner will be such that it inspires trust and confidence and you too will find your success rate to be immensely higher.

Chapter Ten
Giant Power Faith and Belief

"If thou canst believe all things are possible."

-- Mark 9:23

Do you want a really exciting life? Do you want to be admired and respected? Do you want to have an extraordinary life-style? If so, you must release the awesome power which lies inside you. To unlock the power of the giant you have to have faith, faith in the system, the products, and the company even when the evidence may suggest otherwise. Indestructible faith! Awe inspiring faith! Faith itself produces powerful and confident behavior!

There is no power in a weak and indecisive leader. When the fear factor takes over the rest is history. Hope is gone when fear is the guiding light. Fear and faith are natural enemies and cannot coexist! The major fear word is IF. It is the word of delay and despair.

BOB CRISP - RAISING A GIANT 2.0

My friend Dr. Bill Cook tells of the dentist who bent over working on a patient. The patient cried out "Here, Doc, you've pulled the wrong tooth!" The dentist replied calmly, "I know it my good man, but I'm coming to it."

The word "if" destroys talents, wrecks confidence, assails character, robs us of our dreams, and diminishes our bold spirit. Someone once wrote:

> "On the plains of hesitation,
> Bleach the bones of millions,
> Who on the verge of victory,
> Sit down to rest, and while resting died."

Marvelous Marvin Hagler was preparing for his second championship fight with Sugar Ray Leonard when he was interrupted by a reporter who asked him what he was doing to get himself ready for this fight. His answer? "I'm feeding the faith and starving the fear." Such is the way of success in life.

Feed the faith and it will grow. Feed the fear and it too will grow. Someone once said "All are brave when the enemy is gone." Daddy Warbucks in Little Orphan Annie said, "A coward dies a thousand deaths, a brave man only once." What makes us brave in the face of the enemy? Faith! Faith!

All new businesses are founded on hope. Therefore, faith is inextricably intertwined with new beginnings. Dr. Robert Schuller says "When there is no faith in the beginning, there is no hope of ever winning."

The good book says that "As we go, our faith will grow." The power of a consistent faith in our decisions can be awesome. The faith factor then, is the key to creating a continual flow of successful activity in your business.

President Kennedy, quoting George Bernard Shaw, said "Some men see things as they are and say, why? I dream of things that never were and say, Why not?"

Let's examine some of the practical benefits of faith and then take a look at the things which interfere with our faith. First, consider that there are no guarantees in life. None of us know exactly what is going to happen tomorrow. The uncertainty of life itself causes many to live a life full of fear and self-doubt instead of a life filled with expectancy and self-assured behavior.

To be a giant you need faith in your ability to deal positively and successfully with anything life has to offer. Think of all the negative things that have happened to you in the past in school or at work. At the time, you probably believed that you would never make it through, but you did. You passed that calculus class, got the next promotion, kept your job and got a nice raise. If you lost your job you found a new job. You refinanced and saved your house and got a clean slate financially things worked out and chances are you're better off today than before.

You'll do well at things in the future too! Now you have a choice, you can do things with faith or you can do them in fear. What do you think of your chances in either case? Chances are not good for the fear method, right?

BOB CRISP - RAISING A GIANT 2.0

The late Dr. David Viscott, a well known television psychiatrist and noted author, wrote in his book "Risking" that "When we come to a precipice we tend to look down rather than across… but it's the width we must cross not the depth." The challenge with most of us is we look down at the danger and not across at the reward. It's the width not the depth we must jump!

Faith brings us to the brink and gives us the power to find the solutions and act successfully to cross the chasm. Fear, on the other hand, causes indecision and erratic performance. Who would you rather follow into battle, someone that is shaking and quivering or someone whose hands are steady, eyes are clear and whose voice doesn't waiver or shake?

The people in your business feel the same about you. They are looking for any sign of fear and uncertainty. If you don't go to events, they read that as a sign of weakness and indecision. Even if you have a good excuse your group thinks of you as a compromiser and may read your seeming indifference as a lack of faith in the process, products, or people.

Michael Kelly, a friend and confidante who lives in Virginia, and incidentally one of America's greatest communicators, says "Ignorance on fire is better than knowledge on ice." Right on brother! You see, faith lights the fire in our lives even when we are not well trained or when we are ignorant of all the proper and correct things to do we can exhibit faith in the process. And let that faith light a fire in us. Just because you can't sing doesn't mean you can't have a passion for music!

Finding Fire in Faith

Shortly after I entered network marketing my sponsor, who was from South Carolina, told me that I needed to get some "far." Far? What's far? He said "Far, you know like what's in the farplace." I said, "Oh, you mean fire?" He said "That's what I said, far." He said, "Crisp, if you ever get on-far (one word) people will come from miles around to watch you burn." I wondered then how you catch far (fire)? I found fire in faith! If you want your fire lit, try faith! When faith walks in, fear walks out. Someone described fear as "the dark room where our negatives are developed."

Some people say "You are what you think about all the time," I know that can't be true because if it were, I'd have been a girl by the time I was fifteen. So just thinking about faith won't fill you with faith. Faith is an activity, not a state of mind.

People today more than ever are looking for people of faith to step out and lead the way into the very uncertain future. People who are "on far." Fear impedes the way. Fear makes the strong weak. The knowledgeable are rendered helpless under the weight of fear. President Franklin Roosevelt once decreed, "The only thing we have to fear, is fear itself." Do your actions and words inspire faith or fear? Are you a part of the faith solution or the fear problem?

When faith exists, the organization moves confidently ahead. They can march together and overcome insurmountable odds to accomplish their objectives. When fear is the password, then the organization stands still, questions every detail, scatters to fractured groups and loses its focus.

The Power of Stories

Stories of successful people who have overcome similar challenges to yours inspire faith. That's why I recommend a steady stream of "story CDs or DVDs" in any progressing network marketing group. Listening develops confidence. This confidence validates our initial decision to get involved.

We all need to see and hear what others have done in similar circumstances, we then are inspired to a greater faith in ourselves. We need to hear from people who, just like us, have made the trip up the mountain and instead of pulling the ladder up behind them have held it for us. Their lives and courage inspire us to go on!

One person with vision and faith can move others to act when logic cannot. Remember this admonition "Man is more convinced by the depth of your conviction than the height of your logic." A leader must stir our blood, not appeal to our reason.

Visual and auditory stimulus which inspires our faith is far more valuable to us than product seminars which may in fact only inspire us to more questions and inaction. Have you ever met someone who knew everything about the product but didn't sell anything? Or someone who could give the entire marketing plan better than anyone else, yet never sponsored anyone? Of course, we all have met people like that. These people were frozen by their fear. Their self-esteem and confidence is gone. Fear is the biggest killer of dreams ever!

Your mission, should you decide to take the assignment, is to seek and destroy the fear! How? By living a life of faith yourself! Advance confidently and in full knowledge that you and your organization will deal with the future better than the past. Faith increases with action! Conversely faith decreases with inaction.

I am asked frequently what are you going to do if the business doesn't work or doesn't last? The answer I give is simple-we'll do something else. A lack of confidence? No. On the contrary, it shows confidence in myself and the future. No one can be certain that a company will last or that everyone will make it, but we can have faith in the process of faith itself and approach the future with confidence and assurance. When I'm asked if I can guarantee that the business will still be around tomorrow, my reply is, "Will you still be around tomorrow?"

I'm not trying to suggest blind faith in all things. I'm not suggesting that there are not some charlatans out there preying on the innocent or that there are not some businesses that take advantage of people. I am suggesting that you get your questions answered before you start and then give it all you've got. Remember that nothing is perfect!

"Do the thing you fear the most and the death of fear is inevitable."

■ Napoleon Hill

If it's worth your time, it's worth your faith driven best!

Bob Crisp - Raising a Giant 2.0

Don't save your best-give your best!

Chapter Eleven

The Giant's Friends... The Upline Powerline

"Two are better than one; because they have a good reward for their labor. For if they fall, the one will lift up his fellow; but woe to him that is alone when he falleth; for he hath not another to help him up." -- Ecclesiastes 4:9-10

You are going on an incredible journey and you are going to need a guide. The fact is you are going to have plenty of company. If you have done your homework correctly and your upline "due diligence" you will have the assistance of many of those key players. Getting connected to those key people early will help you in your run to success.

In the thirty or so years I have been involved in the network marketing industry there have been many changes. The most obvious changes have come in the number of network marketing professionals that are around. By and large these are talented people who have a long term vision of the industry. All of them have one thing in common, they started out just like you!

Network marketing professionals have the ability to communicate with others. Many have a huge network of followers. On the other hand, there are many pretenders

BOB CRISP - RAISING A GIANT 2.0

and hangers-on who would like you to believe they are professionals and have immense skills while in fact they are weak and inefficient. It takes time to become proficient at leading large groups. I was in the industry five years before I realized how really difficult it was.

Today we have a large number of "flashes in the pan" who believe themselves to be network marketing giants just because they have a large income. Prince (the rock star) may have a large income, but he probably knows little about the record industry.

While you should not be too cynical or skeptical about your sponsor and upline players, it pays to do your homework. Many enticements may be given to recruit you but bear in mind few recruiters really deliver their promises. There are some things to look for and some key questions to ask that will give you an indication of what to expect from your upline.

Evaluate the people you will be learning from and working with. What is their experience level? Talk to others who have known them and worked with them. Act as if this were the most important decision in your life. It may well be.

Circumstances in the business change daily. Newer recruits with skills and desires more or less than yours may change your upline's expectations and cause them to modify their work schedules. Your schedule too will change as you see new and talented individuals come into your downline. You must be flexible. Play the odds and keep your focus. Expect a miracle everyday but don't count on them… and be patient YOUR day is coming too!

Evaluating the Talent

I classify players (people/distributors) into three basic categories -A, B and C players. The 'A' player is the lead player in your upline. They establish themselves through work habits and leadership activities. An 'A' player does most of the events coordinates the downline activities and focus.

The 'B' player on the other hand is usually a distributor who is in 'A' player training. He or she may do your events, three-way calls with you or your downline associates, provide home event support to downline and carry out policy and activities.

The 'C' player is usually no more than an "inside" center-of-influence. The 'C' player is officially a distributor but provides minimal contributions to the daily activities of the business. The 'C' player rarely goes to events, never does an event himself and wouldn't know how to do one if asked. The 'C' player can play an important role because he/she is your link to another list of prospects and by "getting in" the 'C' players have put their stamp of approval on the business and have become a real positive asset. Don't expect active help from an upline 'C' player.

Your first order of business should be to survey the people in your immediate upline and evaluate who will best relate to you and your prospects and who is best suited to help you get started. Find and get to know the 'A' players and remember they have experience in putting together networks rapidly. Hopefully, you have some of these people in your upline payline.

You will want to know some important things about the players in your upline. Who is the most experienced in network marketing? What kind of companies have they been with in the past? What are their strengths and weaknesses? For example, do they have good telephone skills? Are they good public speakers? Are they good trainers? What have been their past successes? Do they take initiative? In other words who is the leader and how do you get their attention and assistance?

Obviously, you can succeed in network marketing without help from anyone in your upline. I know several people who have done quite well without an ounce of help or communication with an upline. However, the odds are against you and in today's highly motivated marketplace it is important to establish some credentials before committing time and money to an enterprise.

Watch out for a string of consecutive 'B' or 'C' types in your upline. This makes for sporadic if not non-existent training and assistance. It's better to get no help than the wrong help. A good rule of thumb? You should know everything you can about those in your upline who are going to be paid on your sales volume. This will arm you with the confidence that you are a valuable asset to them.

The first order of business is to get the telephone numbers of the people in your upline all the way up to the company if possible. Your sponsor should be able to give these to you. If not, keep calling upline until you compile them all.

Second, if possible, schedule personal individual interviews with each of the key people in your upline. Take along your prospect list and a month-at-a-glance calendar. Be prepared to tell your upline the extent to which you are willing to invest time and capital into the growth of your business. Have a schedule in mind to get started.

What should you expect from your upline? How much and what kind of help should your upline give you? The answer is not simple. The level of help you can count on depends on a myriad of things. How many legs does your key upline player already have? Are you in a key position in this player's downline?

The problem is evaluating the value you are to the players in your upline. Are they trying to qualify for the next recognition and pay level? If so, how will your success impact that qualification? Also, bear in mind that as in most things in life, the "squeaking wheels get the grease." The louder you shout the more likely you are to get the help you desire and deserve.

Remember, the business is built with people just like you and you must establish your value to entice the upline to work with you as opposed to someone else who may have demonstrated a deeper desire or willingness to work than you. Your value to your upline will be directly commensurate to the level of their need combined with your commitment.

From my experience, I look for those who ask for help, those new distributors that set up events for me to do and communicate their desire for help enthusiastically. I

Bob Crisp - Raising a Giant 2.0

don't work with people who won't go to events (today online webinars and conference calls) unless I know for sure I'm working with a high quality 'C' player. I look for those who go to events regularly, show up for every training event, and listen to CDs daily.

Your upline should be concerned with building depth in at least one of your business legs (their business also) well beyond their pay line. In addition, if you are working with knowledgeable people, they should be concerned with working diligently in other legs within their payline to maximize their monthly profits.

If your company's pay plan pays through five levels you should of course be able to count on the help of at least five upline team-builders. But which ones do you ask for help and how do you get their attention? Evaluate who you want help from based on what you've learned from the previous chapters.

Getting the help of your key upline leaders is a matter of understanding what's in it for them and how your abilities and commitment exceeds the other alternative options where they could be putting their time. What are the possible motives of your upline? Remember that these same motives will apply to you as soon as you have a significant downline organization. (Also always bear in mind that what you do to your upline will inevitably be done to you by your downline.) Now that we've got a fix on the problems let's look at some reasons why upline should help you rather than someone else.

Influence, List, Ability, Commitment, Timing

First, I look for someone who is dedicated to success in the business. I evaluate the new distributor's prospect list. What type of people do you know? Who have you left off your list? Is your Doctor on the list? How about your dentist or insurance agent, pastor or attorney? Are you a person of influence or are you a developing networker?

By "influence" I mean someone who has a regular interaction with those on his list. Do you have a close, interactive, current, relationship with these people or are you a distant relation?

The impact of your list, the intensity of your commitment and the skills you possess or the dedication with which you approach the business will greatly impact the amount of time your key upline will be willing to spend with you directly.

Note: You may well be better off being sponsored by someone who is less successful rather than a super star whose time may be in more demand by other members.

The key issue as to whether you are in the right spot in the line-of-sponsorship will be the type of help you need. If you need someone to contact and invite with you and do a lot of hand-holding in the early stages, then you might want to be sponsored by someone of lesser stature. On the other hand, if you are skilled at contacting and inviting but need more advanced guidance and counseling from time to time, you would be better served being sponsored by an industry veteran ('A' Player).

The best of all worlds would be to be sponsored by a skilled communicator with plenty of time to work with you and your new distributors who is in turn sponsored by a successful industry veteran. Your sponsor would be a good 'B' player and the four or five next upline, stronger 'A' players.

The people in your upline can be of value in indirect ways too. Their story of becoming a success in your business or in the industry may serve you well. Learn the success stories of the key people in your upline business. Thus you will always be able to point out to your downline the power in the line-of-sponsorship, and the help possibly available to those who are serious about the business. In the recruiting process you will often be asked about the quality of help your new distributors can count on from your immediate upline. It is an invaluable asset to be able to proudly point to your upline's success.

In network marketing your new job description may well be described as a "paid professional story teller." I was talking to a "Wallstreet Wizard" the other day who told me that the most important thing in every new public offering of stock was the company story. In other words, where has this company been? Where are they now? Where are they going? To be a great story teller you need to know the past, the present, and the future of the subject. The better you get at telling these stories, the more successful you will be.

Bob Crisp - Raising a Giant 2.0

Your upline can be the difference between it taking forever to reach your objective and reaching it in the desired amount of time. It is rare when someone becomes successful in network marketing without the help of a strong and effective upline. The relating skills of your sponsor, their social skills, the personality mix, the upline maturity and experience all combine with your own skills and experience to determine the speed at which you will develop. Every day is a new day and the results are based on this delicate mix.

Get to know your upline. Build a strong relationship with them. Pay attention. Put away your own ego and learn the way it's being done before trying to put your own spin on things. The key to success is duplication not innovation.

The journey after all is more fun when you take along some old friends as well as some incredible new ones. Get on the way now. Don't procrastinate and put off the decision to act. Call upline and say, "I'm ready to go and I'd like to have an hour of your time this week to discuss the best strategies to reach my objectives."

My sponsor was perfectly suited to nursemaid me through the first few indecisive months of my network marketing career. He was patient and loving. He encouraged without badgering and made sure I was aware of the help that was available to me if I would accept it. He was however, a 'B' player, meaning I had to look beyond him to someone who was more involved in the leadership mix of the company and to whom I could seriously identify.

I soon outgrew my sponsor's ability to help. My skill levels were higher and my commitment soon became deeper so I had to look upline further for help. This is not an uncommon occurrence. You too may find the need to look upline for a broader base of knowledge. Be thankful for a sponsor who will introduce you to the concept and lead you to those who will teach and train you to go on to world-class success.

While I advanced more quickly than my sponsor, I could never claim to have done it without his very vital help during those first few critical stages. I am grateful for a friend who cared enough to care enough.

Perhaps that is why people in networking are fond of saying… "People don't care how much you know, till they know how much you care."

The new age of the internet has given us a new vehicle to "Stay in Touch" so why not resolve to get better at it? As a matter of fact, why not master it today?

Chapter Twelve

Symptoms and Diseases - The Real Causes of Failure

"The block of granite which was an obstacle in the pathway of the weak becomes the stepping stone in the pathway of the strong."   -- Thomas Carlyle

The network marketing business is a grand and glorious thing. It provides opportunity where none existed. It allows each person to succeed or fail largely on their own merits with no free rides! Inevitably, however, the negatives creep in, diseases which may not seem important or life threatening in the beginning, but when left un-treated become cancers which destroy.

Where do these diseases come from? Diseases that keep us from realizing our dreams and goals? We've already discussed the power of faith and the destruction that fear can bring. Those are inner things, which in fact, spawn other potentially devastating activities. In this chapter we will look at some of the more common
and deadly business diseases in network marketing.

Companies have been known to reach hundreds of millions of dollars in annual sales volume only to come crashing down in shambles. Once high rolling distributors with six figure monthly incomes find themselves broke and back where they started. Why? Why do so many high flyers take the big fall? (In the last chapter I will discuss my own fall)

Why don't companies continue to grow? What happens to cause such colossal collapses? To find the answer we only have to examine the foundation or culture of the company or organization. We will usually discover that the culture was ill-designed or non-existent and by the time anyone realized the company was in trouble, it was too late to do anything about it.

The signs were there all along. The company brass and field leadership however, were too busy spending their money and basking in the glow of their success, while indulging their enormously over-inflated egos, to pay attention to what was really wrong.

In America we love to treat symptoms and ignore the diseases altogether. Thinking many times that the cure is going to be worse than the disease; we sweep the facts under the carpet and hope and pray for the best. We sow the seeds of destruction then hope for a crop failure!

Treating and analyzing symptoms gets to be a habit. For example. Let's say your overall new distributor sponsoring is down. Is it because of a natural cycle or is it due to something you did months ago that is now surfacing to bite you in the backside? How do you know when and how to react? What are the signs that you are in big trouble versus just going through a phase?

Sponsoring may be off because you are focusing on volume. You may have taken your leaders out of the field for an event or retreat. It may be that you have reached the pinnacle of a sponsoring boom and are adjusting to a more reasonable sponsoring curve.

However, let me caution about being too naive about the fall of the sponsoring rate. Usually the first thing to go in a network marketing business is the reduced sponsoring rate. Did the curve fall dramatically or slightly? Have you been at odds with a major distributor?   Have you secured your influence in depth under him or her?

The network marketing business is not very resilient. Contrary to what most veterans may believe or teach, credibility is like virginity, you only get it once. Once the credibility is gone the party's over. What do you do? Go sponsor some new people and build again. Don't wait for the dead to resurrect. They may never ever get the vision again. On the other hand full-timers, those with higher incomes and bigger downlines, must not be too quick to throw in the towel.

All may not be lost. What's needed now though is not a treatment for the symptom, which is lack of sponsoring. What is needed is a shot in the arm for credibility. A new focus on something different and more dynamic is essential. For example, a new face to follow, a more powerful and convincing rallying cry, a theme that inspires, or a diversion that may issue a new call to action.

Bob Crisp - Raising a Giant 2.0

What do most companies do? The first thing most companies do is change the marketing plan thinking that more money to the big shots will make it all better and keep them around. The bonus plan was good enough to get you where you are so why do you have to improve it now?

According to Professor Fredrick Herzberg "acceding to pay and hours or company policy provides no on-going or permanent motivation." If the solution or cure for most of the ills of a descending network marketing company is not more money, what is it?

The answer according to Herzberg is in the realization and satisfaction of our hungers for recognition and self-realization. Why did the Branch Davidians stay with their crazed leader? The psychic satisfaction. The nature of man is to seek to be fully and completely reassured of his permanence. Security, recognition, a sense of belonging to something bigger, even if it means pain today, will give us renewed hope for tomorrow.

Go back to the foundation of the business. Were there systems in place to train and nurture leaders? Probably not. Most businesses are one dimensional "sponsor and sell." Got a problem? Business down? Is sponsoring off? The common reaction is? No problem! We'll just run some promotion, offer a bigger commission and bingo! Sales will return to normal and sponsoring will climb once again.

Not true! Band-aid cures for deadly diseases rarely work. It's like trying to balance the tires of a car while the car is going down a freeway at 70 miles an hour. Impossible! Just as you can't put toothpaste back into the tube, you can't nail jello to a wall or dribble a football neither can you get people who have lost their faith in the products, company, or upline people to believe again!

When new distributors fail to sponsor, is that a symptom of poor training, poor leadership, poor products, outrageous pricing or what? The answer almost always is in the initiation process for new people. Usually it's not lack of training. It's lack of the right kind of training, training that's tailored to new people. Does your program appeal to the majority or to the minority? In other words, since 85% of the population is blue collar or non-professional, does your program cater to the well- educated while ignoring the bright, moderately educated but ambitious?

So you say "sales volume is down and my commission check this month was smaller. Why? What's wrong?" (Maybe nothing) Sales volume is most often the poorest way to judge the condition of the business. Panic sets in far too often because sales drop and thus commission checks fall. This is a natural cycle. (Assuming that at the same time sponsoring didn't drop too)

When the focus is only on sponsoring at large rates you can produce some very unreal and unsustainable numbers. The industry average is less than $100 per distributor per month in volume, yet it is nothing to see companies under five years old averaging $1000 or more. The more mature your company, the lower the average will be. The longer you've been in and the more distributors you have, the more your average will be reflective of the whole.

Bob Crisp - Raising a Giant 2.0

New distributors tend to buy more products for demonstration and personal use than do older, veteran distributors. That's why sponsoring is the life blood of the business. Incidentally, the life insurance and real estate industries couldn't survive a day without the new recruits who expand the agency network and sell life insurance and real estate to their spheres of influence and "inner circle."

Over-reaction will kill a group faster than under reaction. The old adage "if it ain't broke don't fix it" applies. Too often the quick trigger shoots the wrong guy and many times the good guys get hurt more than the bad ones. If you want to avoid long term disaster cut out the "bad guys" before they cause you damage.

Be careful however, not to confuse personality conflicts and differences in style with truly damaging performance. It's what you "do" that makes the difference. Don't see those you disagree with as bad guys simply because they don't do things your way.

Identifying the bad guys may be harder than you think. Basically, those who sponsor people and leave them high and dry without training and without assistance probably do more damage than more overt offenders. Misrepresenting the potential of the marketing plan or overstating the value of the product is two of the more common bad guy offenses. People who promise more than they are willing or can deliver are always a problem.

The streets of the world are littered with the bodies of the hopeful who if they had been given half a chance could have made good distributors and provided long-term stability for a good company. Instead, they wound up bitter and sometimes broke because nobody cared enough to make good on the promises made when the new distributor entered the program.

Treating the diseases that attack the body of a network marketing group is a matter of treating the fears, frustrations, inhibitions and ambitions of people. No one succeeds alone. As John Donne said, "No man is an island unto himself." The problems that plague the network marketing industry like most other industries, governments, and organizations are people problems.

Finding a quality mentor is the most important thing we can do in life. I don't know what I would be today if it weren't for mentors who have put up with my temperamental behavior and loved me through the tough times. Patience, a virtue I find terribly lacking in myself, is a healing balm to most of us who need an extra measure of help.

Fixing problems that don't exist by misreading symptoms for illnesses is a common mistake. Man is motivated from within as well as by material external things. The person who is "fed" today will be hungry again tomorrow but the person who is "led" today will be a leader tomorrow. Self-realization and actualization is far more lasting than a bowl of rice. Not to diminish the need for physical food and material gain, it is just that I have found that we never know the real joys of being alive until we go beyond the physical to the spiritual or inner self.

The baby may not be crying because he or she is hungry or wet, maybe the child is crying out to be touched or held. Your group may not be stalled out because the products are not selling. Your group is not selling products because they are stalled out. Running a sales campaign may not be the answer to your problem. Most of the time groups stall because of personal problems, a breach of integrity or miscommunication.

Disinterested or indifferent leadership brings about disharmony and usually produces a blasé' attitude towards the business. Have a party. Get to know the real people behind the faces in your downline. Few people really know anything about their neighbors and business associates.

How well do you know YOUR TEAM?

Can you name the children of your top 25 distributors?

How about if they have a pet?

What's the color of the living room carpet in their houses?

Could you find their houses without instructions or an address?

What month were they born?

What did they do for a living before joining your team?

What state were they born in?

Where did they go to school?

Are they internet savvy?

BOB CRISP - RAISING A GIANT 2.0

These are common questions any good friend would know the answer to. How well you know your key people may be the difference between them staying or going somewhere where they will be appreciated. It is the little things that make the difference.

Try building friendships without hidden agendas. Be objective, put yourself in their shoes and consider their feelings and needs first. You'll be surprised at the results!

The solutions most of us seek are short term band aid type solutions which do nothing more than cover up the injury and hide it from sight for a short time. When recruiting and sales are down look for the real reason.

To corporate readers: Don't start messing with the bonus plan and changing the product line until you take a good look at what you are not doing with the business you have.

Finding out what's really wrong is a matter of listening and building relationships. Never assume upon a friendship that is new. Don't take your distributors for granted. Someone else out there will nurture them if you won't. Try sponsoring someone in the Amway business into another company. You'd probably be more successful teaching a pig to sing. Why? Amway distributors use a system of working with people that works, not every time, but often enough to make them the largest network marketing company in the industry!

Keep your eyes on the people. Offer much but always less than you give. Always give more than you promised. And please try to remember their names! Don't be indifferent! People will come out of their cocoons when the world they live in becomes safe. Be a part of the bigger picture. See the real problem and opportunities it presents. Treat the disease and not the symptom.

THE NEW METRICS

Today, in the age of the internet, complex algorithms and metrics can show so many things heretofore hidden or nearly impossible to track. When sales go down, usually it relates to a reduced effort. The signals of which can be marked by reduced sponsoring growth months earlier.

In the past home office staff and field leaders had to rely on "best guess" strategies to identify the problem and to craft strategies which are born out of real information rather than gut feelings.

Most network marketing companies have "Replicated Websites" but do not provide "Analytics" or back office statistics to field leaders… such as "Hits, Video Views, who looked, when, for how long?"

If I can look at website hits and see the hit curve going down I can predict the outcome and therefore do something preventative or remedy the real problem instead of guessing.

Chapter Thirteen
How to Have Power-Packed Events!

>It is a fine thing to have ability, but the ability to discover ability in others is the true test. -- Elbert Hubbard

Oh no! Not another event? We've all heard that one. No one likes going to events all the time. Yet the network marketing industry is all about events and functions. The network marketing work week is filled with events - one to ones, hotel events, conference calls, online webinars, planning events, training, leadership advancement and development events - nothing but events.

For our purposes we will divide this chapter into a study of three types of events. They are opportunity events, training seminars, and leadership development functions. In the chapter on recognition we will deal with the type of events commonly known as "rallies."

Since we spend so much of our lives going to events it is imperative that we make the most of them and make them fun and informative.

When staging events you should realize the "entertainment factor" involved in successful communications. Then events will be fun. When events drone on and on they are going to be marginally effective if not entirely ineffective and damaging in the long run.

Those that have heard me speak know that I punctuate all my seminars and motivational messages with large amounts of humor. Psychologists tell us that the average adult attention span is no more than ten to twelve minutes. If that is true, and my experience tells me it is, then every hour or so a listener takes at least five mental vacations during which nothing the speaker said is heard or remembered.

Any effective platform speaker can tell you you've got to keep it interesting and have plenty of material to attract the audience back from their vacation. I like to take the audience with me on a mental vacation every ten minutes or so.

Boring events are bad for business. Remember your distributors are volunteers not employees. They have to want to stay and to want to come back. The objective then is to "entice and entertain" as well as "inform and motivate."

I. Recruiting Events

Opportunity events should give the established distributor a lift, be fun to attend, and should be staged so that the new prospect is given enough information to make an initial decision. Remember that long after they have forgotten what you said they will remember you and HOW you said it.

Internet Note: Carefully staged web-based events such as "webinars and podcasts" may be the most effective type events in today's fast paced world. Make sure you are up to speed on how to use these dynamic opps to spread the word about your company to a vast audience. AND use Social Media such as Facebook to spread your message.

Power-packed events rarely happen by accident. They require planning and advanced preparation. The key elements are the venue or site, the stage itself, the speaker or facilitators, and the content of the event itself. An opportunity event should do three things… In THIS order of priority…

1. Re-sponsor the people who are already in.
2. Do an attitude adjustment on the group.
3. Provide adequate information for new people to make an informed decision on whether or not to get in.

A. *Location*

I've always believed that events should be held in the best place available. Weigh the cost of the event place against the revenue you expect to generate and determine how "upscale" the event site can be. The better the facility, the better it will be for you and your business. Take into consideration parking and safety factors. A top flight event site lends credibility to your business. When you use a dump or cheap facility it reflects on everyone.

Sometimes it is unavoidable to use lower cost event

sites but you should always strive to go to the upper end of the facilities available. As an example, a Hyatt Regency Hotel would reflect more positively on you and your business than say a Motel Six. (Nothing wrong with Motel Six, I've stayed in my share of them but it is not an "image" builder)

Next, be certain to find out who's going to be event next door. I can't tell you how many times I've had to compete against a dance band or noisy bar next door to event rooms. It's better to postpone the event than to ruin it with an event room next to a loud and distracting party.

B. *Staging and Ambiance*

Note: I am amazed at the total lack of "Production" sense that most event leaders display. You should sit in every angle seat in the room to see if sight lines are good… have someone stand center stage and see if you can see their face clearly… don't sacrifice lighting for a video screen or PowerPoint.

Lighting is a key element often overlooked by those staging events. The speakers face and the chalk board or easel the speaker will be using should be well lit. Elevate the stage or use a riser for the speaker for crowds of over fifty people.

Air-conditioning is vital for comfort. Chill the room down so that when the audience arrives it will not be too hot. Hotels only have two temperatures for event rooms too hot and too cold. Go for the too cold side. An audience that is asleep will never hear the message!

Attractive banners add to an events prestige and visually identify your company. The banner should fit the occasion and slogans and themes should be saved for a leadership or "in group" training. Buy velcro CDs to use to attach banners so that putting them up and taking them down won't take so long. Note: There are some very attractive new displays that roll up in their own containers… full color… great credibility builders.

Internet Note: Using conference call lines to augment online slides is a great way to take advantage of your upline's superior experience. Webinars that last less than 30 minutes are very effective when coupled with an automated email (emarketing) software solution.

C. *Speakers, hosts and facilitators*

Station greeters at the doors of the hotel or facility as well as at the event room entrance. Practice the "smile and handshake" routines with them until they have developed an "electric attitude." An upbeat spirit should show from the moment the prospect or new distributor sets foot in the door! Name tags are great but smiles and enthusiastic handshakes are more personal. Remember to say your own name every time you meet someone. Don't wait for them to remember your name. If you give yours, they will likely give theirs, saving you the embarrassment of forgetting.

For training events of over two hours, classroom style seating is better than theatre style. If your room is too big for the crowd you expect, you can put everyone at tables and make the room look fuller. No smoking in events should always be the policy.

Music, carefully selected and played at a non-intrusive level is always a good idea. Don't select way out offensive music. Stay with message music or standards that most people love.

D. Content

The host should be prepared to make a brief but exciting welcome and introduction of the speaker. Keep it short. "Hello and welcome everyone. My name is John Jones and I'm your host for the evening. How many are here for the first time? (Acknowledge the response) Thank you! I'm a school teacher in the area and though I've done pretty well I've missed out on some really good opportunities. For the past few months I've been checking out some income alternatives. Thanks to XYZ Company,

I've found the answer to many of my financial dilemmas. Tonight our speaker will be telling you all about XYZ. She's a talented and successful business woman who has a track record all of us would be envious of. Join me in welcoming a good friend and business associate Janet Smith!" Introductions should not be too glowing or they become meaningless.

The introduction should be brief but it should say a lot. It should say that the speaker tonight is successful and that she or he is a friend. This lends your credibility to theirs and provides a basis on which to transfer the bonding process of the event to the speaker.

BOB CRISP - RAISING A GIANT 2.0

One of my mentors told me years ago, "Bob, you've got to plow the ground before you plant the seed." In other words, he was saying that the speaker must establish a bond with his or her audience before trying to deliver the message.

Establishing a link or bond with your audience is a must. It can take a minute or an hour. I have a friend who can walk on stage and in seconds the whole audience is listening attentively and is sitting on the edge of their seats to hear what he will say next. It usually takes me several minutes to warm to an audience and them to me. On the other hand, I know many who never get the audience with them.

Appearance and body language should be open and vulnerable. This is hard for most beginners to do. If you're nervous use it to bind your audience to you by saying something like "I'm really nervous tonight, so I'd appreciate all the help you can give me, ok?" The audience will sense your sincerity and psychologically and emotionally be on your side.

I always take five to ten seconds just to look my audience in the eye and smile. This sets them at ease and makes me feel more comfortable too. Tell the audience something about yourself. For example, I have five children so I'll say, "My name is Bob Crisp and I have five kids, all boys, except four." This usually gets a chuckle and I'm off on the right foot with my audience. Never use ethnic, religious or off-color humor with an opportunity event crowd. It's not worth the chance that you might offend someone or their guest.

Loosen up the audience with self deprecating humor. Get a platform speakers hand book and pick out a couple of good, short, easy to tell jokes and figure out how they could have happened to you. Tell the audience early how you became involved in the business and share your motives with them.

Learn the issues that affect people today such as job security, inflation, health care, vacations, buying a new house and the economy. Relate them to the business you are in. It's called "solution selling" and it is based on finding the prospects need and filling it.

Power-packed events have personal testimonials. I generally don't like impromptu testimonials because you never know who's going to say the wrong thing. I like to pick out three or four distributors before the event to tell their story and review with them the key points to make.

The speaker should never leave the platform or the front of the room. Once the bond is made between the speaker and the audience, it doesn't make much sense to break it by giving up the stage to someone who must start all over with the audience.

A big finish is vital. Close events with powerful "to do" points. The audience needs to make some decisions. Decide in advance what those decisions should be. They may be as simple as saying "There are 3 things you can do tonight…

1. Get in… "I'm ready to go"… see the person who invited you for signup details

2. I Need to know more... stick around and we'll answer questions
3. Not interested at this time... thank you for coming perhaps at a later time you would reconsider?

I have even gone so far as to create DECISION CARDS to pass out at the close. Collect them at the door as people leave or have them give them to the person who invited them and then they'll know how to follow-up later. (You can get copies of my Decision Cards in my Generic New Distributor Orientation Course along with many other forms and ads and scripts I use)

Two Categories for Growth

The business can be divided into two major areas of growth. The first area is "Basic Business Training," what we might refer to as "The Science." The second is "Leadership Development" or what we generally refer to as "The Art." Not that there is not art in the basics but new people can become confused by issues regarding style over substance.

The Basic Business Training is divided into two categories; Basic and Advanced, while the Leadership Advancement Training has three areas; Basic, Intermediate and Advanced.

I. Basic Business Training

Basic training seminars are focused primarily on newcomers. The theme should be "Getting started with power and confidence." The basic seminar centers on contacting and inviting techniques, how to sell the products, and where to look for prospects. It also should be centered on goal setting and building the new distributors confidence in himself, the business, and you! The biggest error most people make in basic seminar work is telling too much.

1. Identify the line of sponsorship for everyone. Go over "insider lingo" such as what an "upline" is, or what "downline" and "cross-line" mean. If your company uses BV (Bonus or Business Volume) or PV (Point Value) instead of dollars to figure bonuses then explain what the relationship is between the points and the dollars.

    2. Define the recognition and incremented bonus or pin levels. Show people how they move up. Clearly define and expound on the recognition levels. Stay away from advanced leadership material. Don't get into problems or negatives. Don't allow yourself to be cornered or questioned openly about something personal or derogatory about the business. If asked a negative question be prepared to say "That's a good question if you'll see me after the event I'll be happy to address it for you, OK?"

    Don't spend a lot of time on paper work. It amazes me how many trainers will spend an hour or so in a basic training class covering nothing but paperwork. My suggestion? Simple. Have the sponsor or first upline knowledgeable distributor go "one on one" with those who need help with paperwork. Nothing is worse than sitting in an event with someone who can't figure out if when the form says "social security number" it means

"my" number? Who else? I know the paperwork must be done correctly. I just don't like taking up precious time boring everyone to cover the weaknesses of a few.
3. The same is true of product information. Product information can be boring and mundane. Get someone who knows about the product to make up "Question and Answer" sheets covering some of the more commonly asked questions. Hand them out at the events and take just a minute or two to review.

   Product demonstrations are important, so involve everyone in the discussion on products but don't let it get out of hand. If your company has a large line of products select a few and have different people demonstrate them. Have a time schedule and enforce it.

   Recruiting and "wholesaling" the product is the basis for the basic seminar. Remember, recruiting is the life blood of your business. When you stop recruiting, you will stop growing. This business of saturation is a myth. (See last chapter) When you place your entire emphasis on the retail sale of the product, you will stifle recruiting and slow the organization down.

4. What about retailing? My answer to you is the same as my sponsor's was to me twenty years ago, "Everyone does a little bit." Just think how much success you would have if all of your distributors serviced ten to twenty customers each

month! Most retail customers will come from the ranks of those you show the business opportunity to who don't get involved but agree to become customers. Some people call these "default customers" but I don't look at them that way. I think of them as preferred customers.

They have some knowledge of what I am doing and are a big part of my inner circle of friends and associates. The first thirty days someone is in they should focus on using and getting to know the product line before they try to retail it. Then they can honestly say, "I use the products and have found them to be all they claim to be."

The initial focus then, is on recruiting a group of wholesale distributors, and then the retail sales will come. In some cases, especially in weight-loss companies, the retail sale may indeed come before the distributor signs up. This is because losing weight can be so dramatic that friends and relatives may look at your results and want the product for themselves. This usually leads to the sponsoring of a new distributor.

Generally however, because of the low entry cost of getting into most network marketing businesses, I believe the "wholesale discounts" to be such a good deal, that most prudent people will sign up just to get the savings.

II. Second Stage Leadership Development Part One

Intermediate Leadership Training is for those who are well on their way. Those being trained should have a beginning group of several distributors and should be experiencing some "growing pains." The focus of this training is to teach new leaders to discover some of the nuances of working with others, to learn how to promote events and product sales, to refine their sponsoring and event skills and to enhance their leadership ability. Intermediate training is not for everyone. There should be a qualification level to attend.

A. **How to get new distributors more involved**

Here I emphasize the team concept. I stress the importance of everybody coming to events and the duplication process. By pointing out that those in the downline are going to "do what you do" you are subtly implanting the duplication thought process to be built upon later on.

B. **How to handle negative or inactive downline**

Here I stress the importance of positive mental images. That we can't wait on others to do it for us but must establish our own attitude at a high level and ignore those who would cause doubt and confusion to creep into the organization.

Getting rid of dead wood is a major activity for this group. Selecting a few good ones to work with instead of shotgunning is vital.

C. Teaching techniques

Stress showing versus telling. I like to field train leaders and emphasize taking emerging leaders to home events and to basic seminars. I like to have them speak about a basic topic such as goal setting or I have them cover insider lingo. Sometimes I just have them tell why they are in the business and share a few encouraging thoughts with the audience. They should begin with the thought "Not long ago I sit where you are sitting and wondered how this new business was going to work for me. Today I can honestly say it is going even better than I hoped for." What a great way to begin an event!

D. Defining objectives and group dynamics

This area of training is grossly ignored. Not that setting goals is ignored in principle but that it is ignored in practice. Take time to have each person write down some specific goals (include achievement levels) while they are in the event.

I have a great NDO Book (New Distributor Orientation) which has a great outline for conducting an intermediate training. You may want to consider something like it for your group.

III. Leadership Training

The advanced training programs should have a focus on building leadership skills. There should be a higher qualification requirement for attendance. The qualification should be tied to a company sales volume or pin level. This training is focused on leadership and in-depth network marketing skills. I cover such topics as…

"Social Media and how it affects your business"

"Teachers Teaching Teachers to Teach Teachers to Teach,"

"The Funnel Concept,"

"The Laws of Leadership and How They Affect You and Your Organization,"

"The Seeds of Destruction and How to Avoid Catastrophe and

Preserve Your Group,"

"THE Group, MY Group,"

"Tapping Into a Larger Income Stream,"

"Diagnosing Symptoms and Treating Diseases",

"Perpetuity, a Life-long Commitment"

"The Stratification of Influence."

All of the above available on my website
www.gobobcrisp.com

BOB CRISP - RAISING A GIANT 2.0

Note: I do not endorse or promote any particular network marketing company and am not interested in being recruited into any company as a distributor. I confine my activities to "Systems" only and my focus is on "generic" training. I am available for events and consulting.

I cover this material in my seminars and will include it in my second book called "Feeding a Giant." For those who have attended my seminars this will serve as a guide to put you on the right trail as you develop your themes and concepts for building a long term successful network marketing group.

Intermediate and Advanced Trainings must be carefully staged. They should be held on a quarterly basis; twice a year in conjunction with another larger function and twice a year as standalone events. I sometimes use a remote location where I can get away for a few days with the leaders and play, plan, and teach. I never miss an opportunity to bond with various emerging leaders and to build stronger relationships as well as expand their vision.

"The speed of the leader is the speed of the group" which means setting the pace in your events. There simply isn't any excuse for a bad event. Put fire and flare in your events with music, PowerPoint's, and great videos. Have a photographer take digital photos as distributors arrive, during events, breaks, and outdoor games, then have them posted to a computer and show them at the close of the event along with some inspiring musical theme song. I've used "One Moment in Time" (Whitney Houston), "My Way" (Elvis), "The River" (Garth Brooks), "Now and Forever" (Carol King) and many more.

Bob Crisp - Raising a Giant 2.0

Note: While "Closing" music should be contemplative and evoke a deeper desire to be more committed to their dreams and goals. "Opening" music should be upbeat and rock the room as should music that introduces speakers and new themes. Long after the words are forgotten the "music" will be remembered.

The music, when heard later, will bring back the feelings and bonding that took place during the weekend function and will create an emotional bond that will last forever. You can buy films and short motivational clips from various vendors to use in events which will liven up your event. Be creative. Use centerpieces for banquets and don't spare the cost when creating a special mood.

I once blindfolded over a hundred people, bussed them thirty miles to a secret event place, had them hold hands and lead each other into an event room where we opened with a powerful video CDs that shook the status quo and made an enormous impact. I've spent thousands on stained glass windows to make a stage appear like a cathedral during a Sunday leadership function. I had everyone take a helium filled balloon outdoors after an event in Chicago and imagine all their fears being placed in the balloons as they let them go in the night sky; their fears and inhibitions floating away, replaced by confidence and power!

I've heard that Mary Kay Cosmetics spends over a million dollars on staging alone during their annual convention in Dallas, Texas. The name of the game is Promote! Promote! Promote! This is an investment.

You will be associated with the places you're seen and the people you hang out with. Do it right. Do it bigger! There is no top, no final best event. The idea is to have everyone leave each event saying to themselves, "This was the best event I've ever been to."

IV. Speakers and Events

Leave the audience laughing and wanting more. Applause is a great way to close. Invite new people to come up and meet you after the event. Make the announcements about future events and finish with a quick story.

I was taught years ago that less is more. Get up, speak up, and shut up. Remember that the audience will forget most of what you say anyway. Have a great opener and closer and you will be thought of as a great speaker. Stage great events and you will be thought of as a great leader.

Record or video yourself and study the mannerisms and speech patterns. I have been speaking for 30 years and still catch myself repeating certain words or phrases. Seeing yourself on camera for the first time can be a humbling experience. The camera seems to catch all the flaws. But what a great study tool for those of us who are public speakers.

Repeating words and phrases such as "you know" or "got me?" or "True? And the most famous one of all is "and uh" are marks of an amateur and are not endearing for long. People in the theatre have a saying "Always leave them wanting more" I think we in marketing should heed that advice.

My father is a minister and tells a story about a farmer who showed up for church one Sunday night after days of rain and floods. Since the old man was the only member of the congregation to show, the preacher asked him if he thought they ought to go ahead with the preaching anyway. The farmer said, "Preacher I raise cattle, when I go out to feed my cattle if only one shows up, I feed it."

Well, the preacher took to the pulpit and preached hell-fire and damnation to the lone farmer for two hours. When he finished he asked the farmer, "Well what do you think?" The farmer replied, "Preacher, if only one of my cows shows up to eat, I don't dump the whole load on him." Be careful not to dump the "whole load" on your audience.

I have been asked repeatedly over the years for recommendations for speakers handbooks and books on humor. The following is a list of some I have used and found to be helpful. I must caution you that the useless material out numbers the useful so you have to dig. You may need to change a setting, tell a story in the first person rather than as it is told in the book. (This is called "speakers license.") Work on them until you've got five to ten you can tell well then add to your repertoire often.

I keep a journal with all my stories in it. I suggest you do the same. Not much in this world is original. I borrowed most of what I know from someone smarter than me. The following list is only a small part of my research material. It will get you started. The more you attend events, take notes, and listen to good speakers, the better your events will become. Like sports or music, speaking is something that takes practice. I got mine in the living rooms and dens of backwoods America.

Today, I speak to crowds numbering in the thousands but I can assure you the hardest crowd I ever spoke to was the ones where it was just me and a hand full of little old ladies. Take heart and go get'em.

Research Books for Beginning Speakers

Braudes Treasury of Wit and Humor (Prentice Hall)

The Speakers Source Book (Zondervan)

Isaac Asimov's Treasury of Humor (Houghton Mifflon)

Know or Listen to Those Who Know (Norton)

Chapter Fourteen
Recognition and Praise

When we treat a man as he is, we make him worse than he is. When we treat him as if he already were what he potentially could be, we make him what he should be.
                                                              -- Goeth

We had just landed in Orlando, Florida and as we exited the jetway there was a handsome couple there to greet us. We were there to speak to their Amway family reunion. ("Family" in network marketing terms means you and your upline and downline distributor group). Bill and Carol (not their real names) were glowing and excited! Carol presented my wife with a bouquet of red roses and walked with her chatting up a storm. Bill shook my hand, hugged me vigorously and welcomed me to Orlando. He told me how excited they were that we had come so far to share our business building techniques. I thanked him and they escorted us to a mile long stretch limousine and took us to our hotel suite a few miles from the Magic Kingdom.

As we were walking to the car I observed that Carol limped quite noticeably. As I looked down at this beautiful, radiant woman's legs, I noticed how perfectly shaped her right leg was, while her left was narrow and straight as a stick. In all other respects she was a knockout. No Miss America was ever more beautiful!

Bill and Carol had decorated our beautiful hotel suite with posters and slogans, an enormous fruit basket was

Bob Crisp - Raising a Giant 2.0

there as was a dozen or so cards from the organization's leaders telling us how much they looked forward to our sharing. Bill and Carol did everything possible to make our stay comfortable. It was almost embarrassing how much they catered to our every need.

Saturday night came and the recognition began. Bill and Carol's upline Diamonds came to the stage while the band played the weekend's theme song softly in the background. The Diamond said to the crowd of some two thousand distributors, "Tonight we want to recognize one of the fastest growing couples in our organization." We watched and listened as the music swelled the theme and waited to hear the name of this outstanding couple. The Diamond shouted into the microphone, to the crowd which was already on their feet applauding, "Now help us welcome our newest achievers, Bill and Carol!"

The crowd roared, standing to their feet and applauding for this young dynamic couple. I sat at the head table and watched a five-year-old boy and his seven-year-old sister as they stood in the front looking at the stage looking up and clapping for their mom and dad. I remembered all the times I had wondered if the critics were right about our business.

I thought of the long and lonely road that this couple had come down, because I too had traveled that road. I watched the host hand this lovely mother of two, a dozen long stemmed sterling roses, and Carol, with Bill by her side, made the walk down the stage runway and out to the front to accept the applause she and Bill so richly deserved. This was her night to be a beauty queen, her night to wear the

crown, withered leg and all. I wondered aloud to myself what's wrong with making a hero out of a
little boy and girl's mom and dad in front of them?

I submit to you that not only is nothing wrong with it we need to do more of it! No Fortune 500 corporation did it for them! No boss did it! The rut system and its 40 year plan for failure didn't do it. It was network marketing and a couple looking for "more" for themselves and their children did it. I stood to my feet with tears rolling uncontrollably down my cheeks and whistled and applauded with the rest of the admiring crowd. I have never felt more alive or fulfilled than when applauding for Bill and Carol that night.

176 Steps to Glory

Just five short years earlier I had sat in the Charlotte Coliseum in Charlotte, North Carolina and watched as literally thousands of distributors walked across the stage to get a moments recognition. For three hours they walked across, a steady stream of achievers. Not me, though. I didn't do anything to qualify to be recognized for not even for the lowest level of recognition. I didn't get it. I couldn't understand why we would waste our time like this. Why, I asked my sponsor, had we driven eighteen hours to watch people go across the stage and say their name?

He said something simple like "Bob, this is what we do the business for-recognition." I probably said something stupid like "Not me, I do it strictly for the money." That night I sat there and watched doctors, school teachers, truck drivers, bankers and people of every race, color, and creed go across that stage and get their applause. But nobody applauded for me.

When my sponsor left me in the arena after the event was over, I sat there until the only ones left were me and the janitors cleaning up at 2:00 AM for the next morning's events. I got up from my seat in the back and began to count the steps down the aisle to the stage. 176 steps! 176 long steps to the center of the stage. I walked up on the stage and stood there alone. No applause. No microphone. No band playing a fanfare or theme song. No spot light to light my face, only me and a disinterested cleaning staff.

As I stood there in the darkness, I closed my eyes and I could hear the band, the applause, and feel the heat of the imaginary spot lights on my face. I knew that there would come a day when that stage would be mine. Eighteen months later I stood there on that same stage and delivered the key note speech to fifteen thousand friends and fellow travelers.

My life had changed so much in those eighteen months. I had grown up. My income had gone to nearly a million dollars a year. Where before I could hardly pay all my bills and my credit cards were stretched to their limits... now, I owned expensive new cars, lived in a new home, traveled first class and had money in my savings account. Life was certainly different. But what caused the changes in me?

I think it was standing there realizing that if all these people were "in" and I was "in" then there were many others who would be "in" too. If someone was going to sponsor them, I was going to get my share. But it was more than that, wasn't it? It was the fact that I was missing out on something important to me. I wasn't being recognized. I wasn't an achiever, yet. I knew I could do it too. All that was standing in my way was me and a few months of hard work.

I asked Mary Kay Ash, the founder of Mary Kay Cosmetics, why she did it. She was divorced and had a small child she could barely afford to feed when she got into a direct sales company. No one paid much attention to Mary. She did well but was not a record-setter, not until she attended her company's national convention and watched as they "crowned" the top sales lady that year "Queen." Mary says she sat there thinking "I could do that." She told her manager, "Next year I'm going to be the Queen" but no one paid any attention to the divorcee from Dallas.

The rest is a matter of public record. Mary Kay became the Queen and went on to found her own highly successful company! Why? **RECOGNITION… RESPECT… HONOR… Pink Cars?**

I discovered that the money, cars and material things meant nothing without the recognition and if I could only have one or the other, the recognition would drive me further than the money or material things. Over the years, I have met some wonderful people but none more wonderful than Bill and Carol. Nothing has touched me more than watching their children look at them and admire them.

I've met millions of people in network marketing but I've never met a winner who didn't respond to the recognition. My upline used to declare "Elephants work for peanuts and people work for pins." How true!

BOB CRISP - RAISING A GIANT 2.0

There is a practical side to recognition. The practical side is that recognition, when properly done, promotes the sponsoring and selling necessary to build a successful and profitable business. Recognition promotes "continuity and stability" in the business. When people work to achieve higher recognition levels, they must learn to work with others.

To get recognition we must learn to give it. Imagine if you will... each person that you meet wearing a message tattooed on their forehead which states simply "Make me feel important."

Sam Walton the founder of Wal-Mart and creator of one of the world's largest fortunes took on Woolworths, Sears, Penney's and all the other more established retailers and beat them by offering the customer a "Make me feel important" option. He stationed greeters at the front door to welcome shoppers and ask if they could be of help.

Sam knew that people like to be recognized and not ignored or insulted. The popular belief today is that society is with-drawing "cocooning" they call it. The truth is, that society may be withdrawing, but it isn't because we don't want recognition or approval, it's because we are taking so much abuse in daily life that there is no alternative but to retreat.

What happens when people are given an opportunity to be recognized? I believe history will prove that people will "congregate" again. They will be drawn where they are given attention and feel safe and "valued" again. They will go where their mundane lives can take on a meaningful dimension and the band will play their song. Look at the karaoke craze! People are getting up and singing songs they barely know in front of people they don't know.   They call this "retreating into a cocoon"? Will ya give me a break here? Someone's not paying attention.

Today they tell me, there are over twelve million people in the network marketing industry. Most are part-timers. Many will never make enough money to pay the rent or take a decent vacation but they will be challenged. They will learn new skills. They will be a part of an active network that can lead them to their next divine appointment with destiny.

Don't tell me people don't want to be patted on the back or that the "only thing that matters is the money" because I know from twenty years of experience the real truth. The legal community or regulators will never be able to analyze the intangible benefits received by those participating on the fringes of the industry. One can't put a value on value itself.

A good friend, who led a start-up company to over 180 million dollars in sales in just a short two years time, once spent 8 years with a network marketing company and didn't make enough money to pay cab fare across town. His reply to the question why? "It was a time of personal growth!" He said, "I met so many incredible people who challenged me to reach my full potential. The experience gave me a totally new outlook and perspective." I guess he is proof that "persistence and determination alone are omnipotent."

Bob Crisp - Raising a Giant 2.0

Recognition levels drive volume. On a monthly basis, if your last week's sales volume does not equal or exceed the first three weeks sales combined, then you're not working your business right. Your organization should be stretching at the end of the month to meet their next targeted objectives. Pin levels represent income levels not the other way around. Generally, higher pin qualifiers make more than lower pin qualifiers. An emphasis on the next pin levels will automatically create a building frenzy at the end of the month.

When this is not happening, the organization is doing a poor job of recognizing the previous month's qualifiers. Since the lowest level of qualification is the building block upon which we build our larger successes, we must have a bold and exciting way to recognize the lower pins. Psychologists will tell you that the reward must be immediate and swiftly applied. Some companies simply wait too long to recognize their achievers and when they do it's far too little and much too late.

That's why I support monthly sales rallies. I have found that a "rally cycle" which begins with local or area rallies in the first month of the cycle, followed by regional rallies in the second month, and followed the third month by major rallies is a dynamic program to get the message out to the masses that we know who you are and we love what you're doing for our company!

Area Events

Let's analyze the cycle-first the area rally. These are locally held events. I prefer having this function Saturday night after a seminar. The reason? Saturday night is date night. They don't hold the Academy Awards in the day time. They hold them at night with spotlights, glitz and glamour! They "dress up"! They even get Jack Nicholson into a tuxedo. Make the monthly event an event! Don't do some tack on recognition as so many do… "Oh, by the way, let's hear it for Jane and Clark" type event. Make it special and meaningful.

The area rallies are manned by local achievers and thus become a training ground for lower level distributors who do the recognition and stage the rallies. Ever wonder where people learn to do the basics? Simple. Provide a "graduated" program for their training.

Things as simple as holding a microphone correctly, getting the audience to applaud enthusiastically for the last distributor recognized as well as the first have to be taught. Keeping the event moving and the recognition upbeat is a skill that can and needs to be learned by all. The area rally is where they learn to
do these simple but vital things.

Regional Events

The regional rally is much different. The regional is bigger and more elaborate. It is staged by combining a number of area rally locations into one. Ideally the area rallies average 150-200 people and the regional which combines 5-10 areas will average 1000-2000 attendees. The budget obviously, is bigger; therefore, the event should be more elaborate and impacting.

BOB CRISP - RAISING A GIANT 2.0

Whereas the area rally may have utilized local talent for speaking, the regional rally is designed to bring in the out-of-town superstar. A big name from far away will always bring out the curious and genuinely interested. Since there are more people, the size of the building and stage are more impressive and therefore recognition at these events is more coveted.

A bigger crowd provides more applause and impact. If you're promoting this event at your area events, you'll want to point out that "All of the future leaders will be moving up and I know you'll want to be included in the new pin winners reception afterwards."

I like to remind new distributors that "their group" will do what they do. If they move up so will their downline. By the way, as a side note never tell your personally sponsored people which of them is the biggest. Keep them guessing. Most of the time a new network marketing group will have one strong leg and the leadership in that leg is a combination of many upline people.

The ego of the lowest level leader usually makes him get in the way of growth. The way to avoid this is not to let him or her know how much of your business they represent. People are always introducing someone to me as "their biggest or best distributor." I know the intention is recognition, but the simple addition of the words "one of my" would suffice.

The Majors

Major events are my favorites. This is when the

biggest pins (highest achievers) get together and provide the ultimate arena for recognition. Bring in a full orchestra or band and have   black tie for men and long gowns for the ladies on Saturday night. This is it! Majors combine Regionals to form an event of several thousand distributors. Only the highest level achievers are asked to host and speak.

 This is a major "move up" time. Emphasize that "New" pins will be recognized. "Outside" speakers are brought in. This is the time when the organization "puts their best foot forward." This is the largest stage for recognition. The recognition here will appeal to even the most highly placed people. Professional athletes and movie stars have told me they've seen nothing to compare.

 Can you see how the cycle works? Areas, Regionals, and Majors, then repeat again. It all has a specific purpose to get everyone involved. The cycle makes all the pin levels feel important but more importantly provides for an orderly way in which the have-nots and lower lights can see themselves in the big picture someday. When you look at a tall ladder that leads to where you want to go, you want to see that the bottom rungs are still there for you. So many organizations cut the bottom rungs off and reward only the big shots.

 The healthy philosophy here is, "I climbed the ladder and now I'm holding it steady for you. Come on up!" not "Well I've got mine, so now that I've got mine, let's see if we can keep you from moving up." The beauty of network marketing is that it treats us all the same. I may need to polish my skills more or learn things you learned before you got here, but if I commit myself to the process and attend the events, take notes, review them daily, take action on the ideas, and then I can succeed too!

Major league baseball's top players earn millions of dollars each year for playing only 162 games. If you and I will play the network marketing game 162 times each year for the next few years we can earn a substantial income too. It's all about events, all kinds of them. After all, it is called "Network" marketing which implies a connection with others. That connection or bond is built around these events.

Large incomes are derived from having built a large network or organization. These networks are reliant upon the gathering together of people with a specific purpose in mind. It is an exchange of not only ideas but emotions and that can only be achieved when people get together.

Even if you don't like to go to events you can learn to like them. You have the power to change your future. It's up to you. If you do it in network marketing, you will learn to love events.

I cannot stress enough the power of recognition nor the importance the truly great leaders should pay to it. At the core of continuity and stability, of motivation and excellence is the part that recognition plays in our daily lives. The most important piece of advice I can give you is to "give it and you'll get it." My mentor said to me "No one has ever seen the limit to what can be achieved when you don't care who gets the credit for it."

When my children were small I took them to some of the most beautiful beaches in the world. We built fantastic sand castles together. Like every parent, I built the castle and they took the credit. It seemed so empowering to them and meant so much to me to see them so proud.

It may be true that a large number of people are retreating into an urban "cocoon" but it is more true that people are looking for a place to feel needed, wanted and appreciated. Put your hands together and stand to your feet, applaud for your neighbor, brag on your kids, your church, your spouse. It's celebration time! If you don't think you have much to celebrate, go to the children's ward of your local hospital or visit a nursing home, you'll think differently.

In the Broadway show "A Chorus Line," the "Director" (a cast member) is interviewing "Applicants" who are standing on stage auditioning for parts in a new show. He eventually comes to a petite, cute, precocious looking blonde... He asks her, "Tell us about yourself… where did you come from?" She responds in a squeaky little voice, telling the producer all about her life in school. Then she mentions her physical attributes and laments that she had not been a very pretty girl and had been eager to 'blossom' into a woman."I couldn't wait until I had all the things I was supposed to have, "she declared from the stage… the audience titters…then she made a profound statement: "The only thing that grew about me was my desire."

I wanted to stand up from my seat in the sixth row and shout, "That's all you need! That's all that is essential to grow.... a great desire!" My experience has taught me that desire is revealed in rallies and functions.   Mary Kay caught the vision of being the Queen.

Bob Hayes was just a little boy from the streets when he saw the great Olympic medalist Jesse Owens and caught the vision of Olympic greatness. Like me and thousands of others, you too, may find your vision stirred at the apex of an event.

Internet Note: Today the internet offers us a real opportunity to recognize our top performers. Even social networking sites may allow us to upload photos or video clips of people coming up the ladder... if your company doesn't do it... perhaps you might consider building a website that includes a daily or weekly blog and update with photo recognition of your top achievers.

The Leader's Mantra...

> *Keep the score...*
>
> *Know the score...*
>
> *Report the score...*

Chapter Fifteen
Perpetuity - Build it Once to Last

I cannot commend to a business house any artificial plan for making men producers-- any scheme for driving them into business building. You must lead them through their self interest. -- Charles Steinway

Years ago, when I was just starting out I heard someone talk about "taking the longer view." They finished their speech with a saying, I wrote it down, carried it with me for weeks, read it a hundred times a day, until it was so ingrained in my subconscious that I found myself whispering it unconsciously it says…

"I will do today what others won't so I can live tomorrow as they can't."

Long term stability is what most of us seek in life. This means having a company that thinks like we think and whose management and ownership concerns itself from the beginning with the implications of long term growth. The greatest perceived benefit of network marketing is the possibility of being able to "walk away" after a time of serious building and have a continuing income. My upline said, "It is better to take a little longer now to build it right than to build it wrong and have to come back later and rebuild it." I subscribe wholeheartedly to that philosophy. Time is everything. We never can have today back. Buy your tomorrows back with well spent todays.

In choosing a network marketing company, it is vital to determine what you want to accomplish. Are your goals long-term or short-term? Are you doing a favor for a friend or is this a serious business effort? It may not be enough that you really like the product and think there is a large market for it. You will want to consider many things.

Deep pockets to withstand potential miscues and regulatory pressures and international expansion… a global footprint, management skills, ownership stability, and philosophy are the most important things you should consider. As we have already discussed in the chapter on "culture," the management team and ownership can have a powerful effect on the outcome of any project or business venture.

Assuming that you have chosen a company with a strong management team and solid, compassionate ownership and that the company has a philosophy with which you agree and identify, and then the only thing that's left is for you to put together your team and live happily ever after.

Putting the glue into an organization so that the organization stays intact over time is the vital missing link in most companies. I should point out some important issues before getting into the heart of the longevity matter. One is that some people in society today are just not cut out to be entrepreneurs. Many have a "take care of me" attitude which precludes their success in any endeavor that requires discipline. They will never and should never step out of the ranks of the employed. They are not bent toward a life of individual financial freedom nor are they suited to a life of entrepreneurial uncertainty.

Entrepreneurs loathe the idea of knowing exactly what they are going to be paid each week. While most need the security of a paycheck to make them feel safe… entrepreneurs see problems as challenges to be solved and relish the task of finding the solutions. The mass sees problems as stumbling blocks and inconveniences which threaten their safety and keeps them from the comforts of their home in the suburbs.

Therefore, the problem with making a study of persistency in a network marketing company is one of deciding first what the parameters are for admission to this particular company and what the factors are that favor quitting over sticking? As we will see later, the first few hours of a distributor's life in a network marketing group usually decides the fate of that particular distributor.

Industry estimates that 80% of the people that quit actually quit within the first 72 hours after they sign up. If this is true, then the time to put on the "full court press" is during the first few hours of the new distributor's participation in the group.

Admit it now not everyone belongs in your business. The selection process however, should occur within the confines of the orientation phase of the business. I developed early in my network marketing career, a New Distributor Orientation program so that we could "indoctrinate and inoculate" our newcomers to our way of doing things.

Bob Crisp - Raising a Giant 2.0

We would nursemaid them through this program and romance them for the first 30 days. We built in "event-after-the-event coffees and receptions" during the month so that we could get to the neophyte before the negative brother-in-law did. The key question to answer with new people is whether they are looking for a lucky break or are they sincere about a real financial opportunity? Identify those looking to work the business and those who are simply inside "Centers of Influence." Identify those you're going to have to carry versus those who will carry their own weight.

Does your upline have programs to cement the new distributors into the group? Does your company send out welcome letters? How does the order entry department at your company treat someone who has never placed an order? Are they brusque and rude or are they courteous and helpful? By the way, I always suggest that the sponsor do a "three-way" with the order entry department of your company for the new distributor's first order. Or walk them through the online order processing procedures. While this may seem a little strange to you it can mean the difference between the distributor becoming a top producer and dropping out altogether.

The "intensive care" concept has made a large difference in the staying power of my groups and those of groups in my past companies who have horrible retention and re-order rates. My company called me after my third year in the business and wanted to know what I was doing that was so special that people wanted to stay in? My reply was "I'm just taking care of business."

Bob Crisp - Raising a Giant 2.0

Taking care of business is a good idea. But what do I mean when I say "taking care of business?" Primarily I mean understanding the nature of people and the fears and frustrations inherent in network marketing. How many people, for example, do you know who have ever made a great living selling soap, vitamins, weight loss programs, skin care products or water filters? Not many I bet!

The majority don't even make enough money from their network marketing businesses to pay the rent. So why do they stay? The answer is hope! H-o-p-e!

Why do people spend literally billions of dollars monthly on lottery tickets? Hope! Have you ever noticed that the bigger the jackpot the more people who participate. A close friend picked me up at the airport recently when the California lottery had reached 52 million dollars. The first thing she said to me was "The jackpot's 52 million. Let's go buy some lotto tickets today!" Now the previous month the jackpot was only 36 million dollars, so I said "Didn't need the 36 million last month, huh?"

It's silly, sure, but that's the way human nature is. Many get into network marketing hoping to hit the jackpot. They're not looking for a career, they're looking for luck. However, today we are seeing more serious business people enter the industry. Why? The economy is forcing people into making moves they should have made years ago. Now they're having to due to massive lay-offs and cutbacks in the corporate bureaucracy.

The Department of Commerce just published some interesting statistics which say that "23 million people will enter the job market by the year 2013!"

BOB CRISP - RAISING A GIANT 2.0

John Naisbett, in his bestselling book Mega Trends, predicted that by the time we reached the late eighties and early nineties this would happen. Well educated and capable mid-managers are being forced into the world of private enterprise. The sale of distributorships and franchises of all kinds are up.

Economist Paul Zane Pilzer points out in his book "The Next Millionaires" that "intellectual distribution" or the distribution of information will be the gold mine of the years 2003 – 2020.

The USA Today newspaper reported that "in 1985 there were 13 million home-based businesses in America. By 1990 the number had grown to over 34 million and today the number approaches the 50 million mark and is rising daily." Americans are going back to the "family business" concept which was prevalent at the turn of the century because of the rural nature of society at the time.

If we understand what drives people and what is motivating them to act in the first place we will be better prepared to meet their expectations and demands. It used to be easier to get by with offering help and giving none. Today if you offer to help you will find yourself in hot water if you can't or don't deliver.

Whereas a decade ago, the strength of the average network marketing distributor was less, today there is a distinctly higher caliber of person entering the marketplace. During good times only the out of work and under employed are prospects. During bad or hard times everyone except the most prosperous are considered prospects.

BOB CRISP - RAISING A GIANT 2.0

The term "people in transition" is popular today… but transition from what to what? Transition from a day job to a business of your own… Technology has made our world a smaller place. I can sit on my veranda and use a wireless phone, have a laptop computer online to the internet, a portable cellular phone or PDA for when I go out, and I am never really out of touch. The highly charged atmosphere in which the world does business is requiring rapid and dramatic changes in all of us.   Those who refuse to change will be swept aside.

A highly efficient and dynamic network marketing group must stay on the cutting edge of technology while emphasizing the "high-touch" nature of the business itself. I know many who claim we have gone "beyond the old rally and seminar system of the past." They claim that "we don't need events and don't need each other." By taking this stance they are denying the history of man, as well as admitting their inability to deal with people on a personal level.

Have you ever sit in a movie theatre and laughed until you cried? Have you watch a touching scene and it moved you deeply? Sure… all of us have… youtube, a big social media site has over 200 million subscribers… an overweight, doudy, middle-aged old maid appeared on Britain's Got Talent and sang a song from Les Miserable "I dreamed a dream" she stunned the audience and the video clip of her singing appeared on youtube the next day… in short order over 103 million people watched her sing… and a new star was born… with all her imperfections… someone will "sing their song" from the network marketing world and it will rock the world… it may be you.

BOB CRISP - RAISING A GIANT 2.0

Internet Note: Bill Gates, the richest man in the world, pointed out in 1991 that the "internet was a dirt road... but had become a 4 lane highway... and would soon become a super highway running from distant points around the world to anyone who had a computer and online access... he said, "The people who build the best billboards (websites) and offer people around the world a value based product or service... would own the world."

Question: How many websites do you own?

Naisbett said that "as we enter the age of 'high tech' we will also see the advent of 'high touch'." The fast paced lives we lead need more reaffirmation of our humanness, not less. The critics would claim that this should be left for other institutions, but my answer to them is "this is where we are spending our treasured resource of time and energy and so this is where we must get our spirits fed!"

Is it possible? Websites, blogs, tweats, and noozles... telling the stories of common people doing uncommon things.

I point out to you that the person who knows the marketing plan and the details of the value of your products but is neither sponsoring nor selling products (which fits about two-thirds of our distributors) is held back, not by lack of knowledge, but by lack of confidence, self-assurance and knowledge.

The programs that endure are the ones where the emphasis is placed on the individual as a part of something bigger and greater. The team that plays together stays together! In another arena, they might say the "team that prays together stays together." Today we need more togetherness not less, but our togetherness must be focused on solutions to both our real and imagined fears. The fear of failure and defeat can be as devastating as the defeat itself!

If you want to built a long-term business you won't do so by force-feeding products and programs down the throats of your downline distributors. You will do so with dynamic and caring leadership. You will do so because you have a program that challenges your people to a step by step process whereby they will become what they need to be to reach their highest and loftiest ambitions.

There can be no success for anyone so long as there is a pervasive fear in the mass that the company or its field leadership is in it "only for themselves." The restoration of credibility is nearly impossible.

Remember the key questions everyone asks when confronted by someone trying to sell them something? Do you care for me? Can I trust you? How will your product or service make my life better? These questions address the issue of character and the moral nature of your business and ideals.

Someone once said, "Money will only make you more of what you already are." I believe this is basically true. There is a common thread that runs through all failing network marketing businesses and that is that they have no incremental, on-going, leadership development programs. They do the basic things well, like sponsoring and selling. They sponsor people by the thousands and sell them a garage load of products but then they leave them high and dry and all alone to learn how to sell those products and recruit and train new distributors. Their philosophy could be described as "Put them in, load them up, and look for more," rather than "Put them in, keep them in, and move them along."

Let's face it. Everyone does not come into your business at the same level. Many are searching and exploring feeling around for high gear in life. Some are in the midst of divorce or have just lost their job and seeking reinforcement for their fractured egos. Others are ready for a great opportunity and are impatient to reach the highest income levels. How do we deal with this menagerie of egos and needs? Carefully, would be my advice.

The road to failure is paved with those who paid no heed to the complex nature of the business we are in. I can't tell you how many "Giants and Legends" of the industry are today dead broke and looking for the next deal, simply because they practiced scorched earth policy in the last great deal they were in. They paid no mind to the small details of individual personal growth and ignored the warning signs which are always prevalent in a decaying and dying network marketing company.

The long term viability of a network marketing group must be centered on programs that address the individual's real needs. The first need is the need to belong. People want to belong. The hit television program "Cheers" was all about belonging. Their theme song even said, "People want to go where everybody knows your name." Belonging to something is important. It defines who you are in relationship to others.

The next need is the need to be recognized. We addressed this in detail in the last chapter. Acknowledgment lets us know we are doing something worthy, that our lives mean something and were not just dust. The third need is the need to achieve. This is manifested in the very fact that those who don't move ahead will eventually drop out. How can you create an atmosphere where people belong, are awarded recognition, and advance?

The words are simple, the application of the words and concepts are complex. It goes back to the foundations of the business. If the owners and initial players are not people of character and good will, if they are not compassionate capitalists and only themselves profiteering from the sweat of others, then the project is doomed.

You, however, can be the impetus for creating a new order. You can reach out to those in your downline and form alliances which bring people of "like minds and objectives" together. Napoleon Hill called this a "Mastermind Alliance." A business may falter but the relationships formed in the business don't have to. You are building the foundations for the rest of your life. You can take these relationships and build another business if necessary, but the relationships are the most important thing!

In a healthy relationship between a company and its field force, the concept should be "together we build for the future." It is the responsibility for the field and the company together to seek out those who can teach and train their people. In the beginning it may be necessary to go "outside" the business for this type of help, but eventually, the leadership training must come from insiders, family members (company or field or both).

The culture of most corporations provides little positive reinforcement for field driven businesses. I naturally lean toward a field driven business. Corporations tend to employ people who are not entrepreneurs or risk takers. They tend to develop and distribute materials that are impotent and for the most part worthless. A committee or council set up to evaluate training and leadership development materials are highly recommended.

Companies should consider taking a remedial position on field developed literature and materials such audio and video cassettes. (Due to the legal climate the exception here should be in literature and materials dealing directly with the bonus plan or products.)

The president of the Southland Life Insurance Company in Dallas, Texas told me "Bob, those that can sell do, and those that can't manage." I have always found that managers concern themselves with "doing things right" while leaders concern themselves with "doing the right thing."

The corporate culture of most network marketing companies is the same as in any other company. However, the way companies treat their field leaders varies measurably. Too much control by those who know little or nothing about the business will stifle and kill creative genius, while too little control over those who abuse the system and belittle the value of others can be destructive.

What is needed is an open and honest exchange by caring and dynamic owners as well as ethical, honest, and compassionate motivators in the field leadership. A company will rise and stay at the level of its strongest leaders. "Con-artists" and "users" have no place in our industry and must be identified and expelled as quickly as possible.

The future of network marketing rests with those of us who have an appreciation for how fragile it can be. Regulators and rip off artists are our natural enemies. The media has a field day with both. The regulators have traditionally depicted the multi-level marketing crowd as heartless and ruthless... a reputation, which for the most part, has been undeserved.

I believe the unethical and dishonest in network marketing to be no more prevalent than in any other industry. How many savings and loan, and banking executives have been indicted lately? Real estate scam artists are a dime a dozen and the Securities and Exchange Commission has their hands full trying to keep up with the "fly-by-night" bogus stock promoters in the world.

This does not excuse those in network marketing who abuse or misuse others, who load up senior citizens with worthless and unsalable products. Those who offer advice on how to manipulate your credit card debt to finance unnecessary purchases of inventory or sales aids need to be dealt with. We must be vigilant to be assured of the future of our industry.

The high pressure promoters whose philosophy is "get in on the ground floor now, this opportunity won't be around forever" are usually drifters who have no intention of being around for the long haul. Remember that the termination of a network marketing company usually means that the "last people in" get stuck with products that may be unsalable and with a company whose guaranteed buy-back policy is now no good. These could be your friends, family and acquaintances. They may look to you for restitution or feel ripped off and cheated because you took advantage of them.

    Don't be naive. The business world is dicey at times. Explain the risks involved and be up front about the problems your company may be facing. The good people will appreciate your candor and honesty and will trust you again in the future. Negatives kill enthusiasm so don't be negative. Back-orders may mean your company product is so good the demand is outstripping the supply. It also may mean your company is mismanaged or under financed, so find out before you get angry and splay somebody.

    The largest company in the network marketing world is Amway Corporation who fought a major landmark battle with the Federal Trade Commission over a decade ago. The FTC found in the Amway case "no evidence of pyramiding or scamming." They reaffirmed Amway's own claim that no saturation had taken place even though the company had over a million distributors and had been in business for more than twenty years.

    Regulators constantly attack successful and ethical companies for the unethical practices of a few. They would rather kill the body than treat the cancer. Self-policing is the only way we can have a network marketing industry long-term. Network marketing has a great future if we care for it. How sad it would be to see it go the way of so many other industries. We owe it to future generations to clean it up and make it available in its most worthy form to all who care to enter.

Dream big and act big. Don't dream big and act small. Remember, 200 million people use facebook everyday!

My philosophy has been to "build it once to last." I think you will discover that taking a little more time to pay attention to the small details that address the needs of your downline will serve you well in the long run. When you hoe the weeds out of the garden you will get a higher yield. Cultivating relationships will do the same thing. When the harvest time comes, the crop will be bountiful! Trust me on this one.

Give your people a reason to stay and they'll stay. Give them recognition and they'll build. Give them a home where people know who they are and treat them like friends and they'll follow. Perhaps you could send them a personalized video email asking them to come back?

Don't sacrifice a lot later for a little now. Remember the ant thinks winter all summer. The ant will give all that he has to become all that he can be. Don't be like the Old Testament character who traded his birthright for a bowl of soup. Take the longer view and then burn the midnight oil until the job is done.

Chapter Sixteen
Giant Living - Giant Life!

"Life isn't a problem to be solved it is a mystery to be lived." -- John Bradshaw

The general feeling in most households in America today is that of spinning plates. We are juggling budgets, time, and people. We look like the plate spinner at the circus. You know the one who spins ceramic plates on the points of long sticks? He gets several plates spinning at one time and then has difficulty adding to the number of plates because he's always going back to spin the first plates which are beginning to slow down. Keeping all the plates spinning can be a frustrating way to live.

Refinancing ones' home equity has become a way of life in America. Every two or three years the average American family is faced with the same cash flow dilemma- how to make more money to pay off an ever increasing debt burden. It has reached epidemic proportion. No wonder we live in such a highly charged society.

Sometime ago Bill Murray starred in a movie called "Groundhog Day." Rich Corlis a writer for Time magazine wrote an insightful review of the movie. He said, "Most folks lives are like Phil's (the main character) on Ground Hog's Day: a repetition, with the tiniest variations, of ritual pleasures and annoyances. Routine is the metronome marking most of our time on earth. Phil's gift is to see the routine and seize the day."

Bob Crisp - Raising a Giant 2.0

Life doesn't have to be boring. It doesn't have to be metronome like. It can be exciting and different every day. We don't have to be afraid to risk. We can take the initiative and change a rather common place existence into a more fruitful and interesting life!

Network marketing offers an opportunity to leverage ourselves. It is easy to see that once both partners in a marriage are working there isn't much left in the way of more available time to leverage. Therefore, we must figure a way to do more with the little time we have left. This means finding a way to leverage our existing time to free up time in the future.

Network marketing offers us just that kind of opportunity. To leverage our time means involving others. When we involve others, we then allow ourselves to be paid not only on what we do but on what they do as well. This is called "Overrides" ... income for helping others to succeed.

The managerial system in most companies is geared to the same philosophy. Managers or those who take responsibility for overseeing and helping others with their jobs get paid more. In other words, an executive with a large automobile company is really paid an override in the form of increased salary for the job of overseer.

Unlike the typical corporation however, network marketing allows you to determine the scope of your involvement and the pay scale generally has no limitations as it does in most big companies. Big companies have the philosophy that it's possible for you to make "too much money." Network marketing companies exhort you to make as much as you can without artificially imposed limits.

The frustrations abound within the framework of most corporations. You get paid what the job is worth instead of for what you do. If you're a good cop, you get paid the same as an average cop. If you are a good conscientious bank teller, you get paid the same as the bank teller who is lax and indifferent to her job. In network marketing the difference is like night and day.

In network marketing not only do you get paid today for what is done today you also may receive on-going residuals and overrides that increase for what you did today! It's much like record royalties. The estate of Bing Crosby still receives royalties on his recording of "White Christmas" even though it has been half a century since it was recorded. Authors receive royalties on books long after the work of writing the book is over.

Network marketing offers you the opportunity to gain the time leverage that is so hard to come by. How much can be accomplished in a days time? It's anyone's guess, but you now must determine what you're willing to do. When I first decided to write this book I had to determine how many hours each day I would devote to this project. How many pages would I write? How much time would this take away from other important projects?

The most important thing you can do is determine now how much time you will devote to your business. If you owned a McDonald's franchise and friends came to visit you, you wouldn't shut the McDonalds down while your friends were in town would you? No, of course not! So many people think nothing of missing events, failing to return or make important phone calls, ceasing to make sales appointments and so on just because "relatives or friends came over." You must think of your new network marketing business as a business! NO EXCUSES!

    I've worked for myself now for over thirty years. I learned the hard way when I was younger that the "time stealers" were out to get me. Procrastination ran rampant in my daily life! I couldn't get control or take charge of my time. I'd make one excuse after the other, all of which sounded logical to me. Too hot. Too cold. Too wet. Too dry. Don't feel good today. Nobody's buying life insurance these days! My company doesn't understand me. My wife doesn't understand me. Got to get more rest. Got to go to church, (Wouldn't want anyone to think I was money hungry).

    I've made or heard all of the excuses. The fact is there is only one acceptable excuse..... Death. If you can't or won't control your time then it will control you. If that happens you won't like the results. Ok, so why do we have so much trouble getting people to understand this simple problem?

    Consider this. Since the day you were born others have been making your time decisions for you when you would go to bed, when you would get up, when you eat, go to school, go play, do homework and so on. Then when you grew up, your boss told you when to come to work, when you could take a break or have lunch, when and how long you would work, what you would do at work, when and how long your vacations could be. The consequences were dire if you didn't pay attention.

BOB CRISP - RAISING A GIANT 2.0

After twenty years or so of someone else telling you even the most simple things to do, go, come, eat, rest, play, you are pretty much a time management vegetable. No time management skills are required, just do as you're told. Now all of a sudden YOU are the one who can decide NOT to do something if you don't WANT to. My brother once told me that he didn't think he would LIKE network marketing, I told him LIKING it wasn't required. (I have a hunch a couple of ten thousand dollar bonus checks would have changed his viewpoint.)

The fact is, in network marketing you will do a lot in the beginning for a little financial reward, and do a little later for a whole lot of financial reward. The leveraging effect says that when you multiply any number times any other number the result will be greater than either of the original numbers (unless one of the numbers is the number one). The sixth multiple of the number five is over seventy-five thousand!

The results I experienced during my first year were staggering! Initially, I couldn't imagine how anyone could turn down a deal this good. Only $36 to get started and I am in a multi-million dollar business of my own! What a deal! Even though I sponsored eight of the first twelve people on my prospect list, my bonus check my sixth month came to a measly $3.63. Can you imagine?

The next six months however, were quite different. Whereas during the first six months I never went to or did an opportunity event, during the next six months I did one or two a day every day and hardly missed a night in the next five years. For nearly five solid years I did an average of over 300 events! Over 1500 events. This may seem like a

Bob Crisp - Raising a Giant 2.0

lot, but consider if I had worked a job or had a "normal" business such as a restaurant, I would have worked eight hours everyday, five days each week, fifty or so weeks each year for a total of 250 weeks, 1250 days and a total of 10,000 man hours, and for what? A weekly paycheck!

The results of my mere five years in network marketing? Over 200,000 downline distributors, an annual retail sales volume of over $100 million, and an income that was simply more than I could have imagined it could be. I retired the first time at the ripe old age of 34. My banker asked me one day, while nervously tapping the ends of his fingers together, "Bob, when you got into that 'soap thing' (they always called it a "thing") did you think you were going to get rich?" My reply was simple, "No Bill, I was hoping I would get my $36 (the cost of a sales kit) back."

So what did I do for 300 days and nights a year? Well, the easy answer is events. But it was more than that. I became proficient at selling the marketing plan and products my company offered. I drove 96,000 miles during my first year. Much of that driving was to distant places to hear network marketing professionals talk for hours about their experiences and how to sponsor and motivate people. I never missed a seminar or rally held within 300 miles of my home.

I spent many long nights in coffee shops and dingy hotel rooms. I cashed in bonds, sold property, sold my fishing boat, canceled my country club membership, resigned from civic and church responsibilities and focused myself on the road to financial independence ahead. I created a "purposeful imbalance" in my life for a short period so that I could have a better balance to my life long-term.

Normal main street businesses are open six to seven days a week so I figured I should do the same. My goal each week was seven full blown opportunity events. I also used my day time hours to contact business people, meet with new distributors one on one and to prepare for my weekend seminars and rallies. I read every positive thinking book I could get my hands on and listened to every cassette CDs available from my upline.

I was a man on a mission. The mission was total and complete financial freedom for me and my family. It took two years to achieve that and from then on it was clear sailing.

Time is a deceiver. The clock, with its circular format tells us it will be 5 o'clock again in twelve hours and that our time will return to us. It says to us "there will be another day another time." Don't believe it! There is only now! Our freedoms are taken from us bit by bit. Our time slips away moment by moment.

There is a conspiracy of mediocrity that is aimed at bringing each and every one of us to nothing. It takes courage to take charge of one's own life to "seize the moment" and not let our fears win.

The critics will carp and the naysayers will have their day, but the winners will shine…nothing is more powerful than an idea whose time has come. Nothing is more powerless than a person who puts off doing what must be done to make life full and meaningful. Action is power to perform!

BOB CRISP - RAISING A GIANT 2.0

I have a cousin who used to play Monopoly with us as a child. She had a strange strategy for playing. She wouldn't buy any property. She merely went round and round the game-board content with collecting her measly $200 "salary" as she passed "Go." She never won, she just played. I asked her once why she didn't buy property so that she would have a chance to win the game. She said she wanted to be able to pay the rent when she landed on properties owned by others. I pointed out to her that her strategy was a losing strategy, she replied "Yes, but I get to play longer."

Today she is nearing fifty years old and she has a miserable life. She has grown angry and bitter. She expected more but she acted so small and took no risks. She is one of life's victims. Sadly, she is like so many in life who live to survive... not live to live.

Isn't that like so many in life? For years they played just so they could hang on a little longer, never denying that their's was a losing strategy in the end, but hoping for that lucky break that would justify their inadequacy or laziness. Then the day comes when the money is gone. The job is taken away. The inevitable old age creeps in and the grim reaper calls their number. It's such a futile and false way of "living" a slow and painful death.

My friend Jim Rohn says, "When you're on the wrong road, go quickly," a great strategy for not wasting any time discovering your error and allowing you time to correct it. Instead, we go slowly and cautiously, wasting time which could be spent in another more worthy endeavor.

Bob Crisp - Raising a Giant 2.0

Go quickly and go powerfully. There's a giant life waiting for you out there too. Go and claim it! It's yours! Embrace the large life… don't live second-hand.

Incidents change life… I was in the 8th grade… I came home one day to find that my mom had been to a second hand store in the neighborhood that day. She paid 50 cents for me a new flannel shirt… I loved that shirt. I wore it to school the next day and a boy in my class said to me "I used to have a shirt just like that one but my mom gave it to charity," I was devastated… "Charity?" I never wore that shirt again.

Be bigger and be open to more and you will have more…Take charge today of your time. Schedule yourself a full year of activities and rearrange your priorities so that your network marketing business rates right up near the top. When you give the business your second hand time you will get a second hand result. Same action, same result. A guy said to me, "I've got twenty years of experience," to which I replied, "It seems to me you have one year of experience repeated twenty times."

Can you stand the heat? Is the mountain to high? If you think so here are my standards for living large. During the next year do the following:

1. Go to and hold at least 200 opportunity events… these may be online webinars or podcasts

2. Attend at least 12 leadership development events.

BOB CRISP - RAISING A GIANT 2.0

3. Hold 24 "Nuts and Bolts" trainings and receptions for your new downline distributors… online is most efficient

4. Listen to 250 hours of CDs and DVDs or on network marketing and personal growth… if you don't have access to the information you need you can download my CDs and ebooks on www.gobobcrisp.com

5. Put 50,000 miles on your car or some other form of transportation or conveyance.
   (Maybe better to use the worldwide web?)

6. Contact at least one new person each day and expand your network of contacts and influence thru online social networking sites such as myspace and facebook.com

7. Do something each day for someone who can do nothing for you in return this will build your self-worth

8. Exercise and eat right so that you will live to enjoy your new found large way of life

9. Thank God for giving you vision and insight as well as eyesight.

Chapter Seventeen
The Call of the Leader

"Anyone can be up when they're up, but a leader is up when they're down." -- Kay Fletcher

In 1975 I attended an event in Ashville, North Carolina. I met, for the first time, a group of people I would never forget, and was introduced to a concept I had never thought much about before.

Though I had accomplished much in my life insurance career, qualified for every award and attended many sales conferences and seminars, I had never thought of leadership as being "a calling."

I had been a leader in school and church since I was a child. Now I was hearing something I had never related to business before, that leadership was a "calling." I knew being a priest or minister was a calling but I never thought of leadership in business as being a calling. I assumed that leaders were built and promoted but had always thought of leaders as volunteers.

The speaker that weekend related this to us in dynamic terms. He said things like "Anyone can be up when their up, but a leader is up when they're down." He said "Do yourself a favor, sometime in your life find something to be a fanatic about, preferably everything you do." I was mesmerized. He said, "If you can live without it, you haven't got it" (the calling). I knew in my heart I could never be happy being just another face in the crowd. I could see myself as a leader and wanted desperately to prove I had what it took. If you have always heard that quiet voice of encouragement then you know exactly what I mean.

Network marketing has given me the opportunity to grow and expand my skills and influence beyond anything I could have ever dreamed of. You too will be challenged more than you ever have been and you will be equal to the task just as those who came before you have been.

As a practical matter, the growth of the leader in a network marketing business can be slow and methodical or fast and meteoric! I went for the celestial. Patience has never been my thing. I stubbed my toes and my ego many times along the way. I made some silly decisions but I made some excellent ones too. I learned to work with others and continue learning to this day.

Working together, while an ideal worthy of massive pursuit, it is sometimes the hardest part of building giant network marketing organization. So much is to be gained by weaving the leadership skills and work habits of individuals together. It is impossible to build a giant organization without the cooperative efforts of many leaders.

These leaders have egos and pride. They need massive doses of recognition and acknowledgment. As there becomes more substance to the size of the group, thus more money and power available, there inevitably erupts conflict. These conflicts usually center around control and compensation.

I have run into several conflicts with people in both my own upline and downline leadership. These conflicts usually were worked out positively by sitting down to discuss them. They centered for the most part on differences of opinion on who was "in charge" and around sharing the profits and expenses from our various endeavors. Money and ego - the two most threatening elements to the cohesion of a large organization.

The best advice I ever got concerning the development of my role in the building of the business was "let those who can and who will do the job best, do it." The glory jobs may seem the most attractive but someone has to do the mundane and necessary things that make an organization click, things like getting to the events ahead of schedule to make sure the event room is set up correctly. Nothing is more devastating than getting to a hotel and finding out five minutes before the event is to start that the event room has not even been booked or that there are not enough chairs, or the dance band next door is playing so loudly no one can hear the speaker.

The Money

When I first started out I had a weekly event at the local hotel. I collected a small charge of a couple of dollars each from my distributors to help pay for the room each week. Most of the time there was a serious shortfall which I gladly made up out of my own pocket.

As my business grew and the size of the event room became larger so did the weekly shortfall. I asked a couple of my leaders to share the cost and to my amazement they refused, stating that "they had gotten in the business to make money not to spend it."

I was hurt and angry but held my temper and simply said "OK, but there will come a day when these events make a profit and when that day comes, don't come running to me with your hand out." Well, the day did come and soon I had to deal with leaders who believed they were entitled to a share of the profits each week. It was not a very positive time in my life. All of a sudden I had to deal with human nature in a way I was not prepared.

I discovered the "Little Red Hen Syndrome." It basically is this they may not want to help with the work but they will want to eat the bread once you have ground the meal, and baked it into bread. When the dough begins to rise… the lazy will come to eat too.

These were my friends and nothing can come more quickly between friends and family than money. I have learned some hard lessons in this regard. Have you ever noticed how loaning money to a friend or family member usually ends up with you being the bad guy? The same can be true in network marketing organizations.

The company I was with in the industry would come to town and hold events that were free. I would have to charge for my events so I could afford to put them on. Inadvertently, the company made me look bad because my distributors couldn't understand why company events were free but our local organization events were not. Suffice it to say that expenses have to be shared by those who are expected to gain from the experience.

BOB CRISP - RAISING A GIANT 2.0

Negative people always try to keep the controversy stirred up. I have personally stood in line behind well-healed distributors who were trying to get into an event without paying the door charge. I've heard them brag about it later to their own groups. Little did they realize that the day would come when they would be in charge of the event expenses and would have to make up the shortfall. When that day came they would resent anyone in their group who like them refused to pay a small door charge.

Respect is something you get when you give it... lack of it always returns to you in magnified ways...

I figure it like this instead of a large investment of several hundred thousand dollars, I got to "buy my business" on the installment plan, one event at a time.

I remember driving from Tulsa, Oklahoma to Charlotte, North Carolina monthly and paying $5 to get into each event session my upline held at the old Charlotte coliseum. I did so without complaint or question. I was glad it wasn't more and thankful for the opportunity to do my small part to share the cost. I, however, watched on many occasions as locals, people who lived ten minutes from the coliseum, objected loudly about the amount of money "somebody must be making on all these people."

It had occurred to me that someone was making money on the door charge, but I paid to go to sporting events, concerts and shows. They promised no better way of life for me. At least at these events, I was going to get entertained, inspired, and trained to be a better business person. I can honestly say that if anything, I was "undercharged" not overcharged for the events I paid to attend. I have even paid for events where I was the one giving the seminar or training!

Occasionally, I'll make a big deal out of it by hollering out "You mean I get to hear Bob Crisp for only $20? Here's a hundred. Keep the change, he's worth it!" It usually draws a laugh from those standing around that are concerned about the door charge but makes the point loud and clear "that leaders pay their own way."

If you build the business, you will have to accept the financial responsibility that goes with staging large events. Eventually, the investment will pay off for you the way it has for me.

Who's In Charge?

The confused mind says "NO"

The challenges of upline and downline leadership go far beyond the money issues. They extend to the daily influence that each of the stronger leaders exert on their downline.

First, those who insist on absolute control over their groups will eventually drive their groups away from them. No one gets into the network marketing industry just to find out that they have another boss. The end result we all hope for is freedom, not more bondage. None of us want someone lording over us or restricting our movements in such a way as to stifle us. However, anyone can see that there must be some uniform coherent policies. These policies must be implemented and enforced by the entire group. Those who step out of line then will be ostracized and expelled by the group and not by an individual!

The leadership in the group then, goes to the most senior achievers. A Diamond (pick any higher achievement level such as "Presidential Director") who has been a Diamond for five years certainly has more experience and respect than one who just recently qualified. Only a fool would weigh them both with the same scale.

On the other hand the new Diamond has achieved a major position and should be accorded all the benefits of the position including bonuses, recognition, and input. In an organization where momentum has been established, you may find that Diamonds qualify behind Diamonds who qualify behind still other downline Diamonds. When this occurs, and it does so with regularity, the struggle for position or influence can ruin the unity and harmony in an organization and create such a negative environment that the entire organization collapses.

Remember our discussion of "Who shall be the greatest?" The key to having group unity is in the result each of us hopes to accomplish. What most of us want is long-term income and security, correct?

Security comes from stability. In-fighting produces a fear of instability both in relationships and in business. When children see their parents fighting they naturally assume things aren't good and feelings of insecurity arise. We need to realize the danger of a power struggle. Like a divorce, the struggle between upline leaders can tear a family apart. Momentum can disappear overnight.

BOB CRISP - RAISING A GIANT 2.0

Credibility that ran so high yesterday can be dashed in an instant. Before you know it, the security is gone and with it the income to which you had just grown accustomed.

My advice on how to avoid this calamity? Communications. Acknowledge the leaders in your own upline. Don't project leadership on someone who doesn't want it or isn't aware of the needs of your organization. If there is a distinctly higher pin level achiever in the area who wishes to the have the responsibility then it should go to him or her without question. (The exception is when the bigger pin is out of synch with the general direction of the organization or is not capable of doing the job).

Encourage discussion around the subject of "How can you improve what you're doing" and "who is achieving better than average results in the group" rather than "what's wrong with the group and who is doing bad things."

I'm not suggesting a Pollyanna attitude, but I am suggesting a dynamic interaction of solution oriented people. Bellyachers never achieve great results and they are no fun to work with.

Simple things such as hosts, greeters and speakers can be hot spots for jealousy and envy. I have found the tenderest spot of all is who's going to do the speaking. This is both a skill level and a recognition level. Unfortunately, in today's fast paced network marketing industry there is little time to develop speaking skills before someone is thrust into the arena.

The world is full of people who want to go immediately to this level. This is the highest honor and responsibility that an organization can bestow and should go to the top achievers who have paid their dues while coming up. Nothing destroys credibility more than having someone get a free ride while the ones who are doing the work are ignored.

I am always honored to be asked to speak but I am thankful for the role the supporting cast plays so that I can look good. Remember too, that if the speaker looks bad it reflects on everyone.

A leader may be called upon to do many things. I have picked up trash, set up hundreds of chairs, taken money at the door, hung banners, brought the sound system and set it up and done the speaking thousands of times. The real leader leaves nothing to chance. EVER! Good leaders seek a higher plain all the time!

Bear Bryant the famous coach of the University of Alabama football team, once hung a sign over the doors of the team's locker room which read "Be good or be gone." Max McGee who played for Vince's Green Bay Packers, said, "Vince taught us what it meant to stand in the winner's circle, and once we tasted the sweet wine of success we never wanted to go back." Lombardi also said, "It is not enough to be good some of the time, you must strive to be good all of the time."

Life treats ego maniacs and people consumed with power the same. Ultimately, they are brought down. Save your ego and follow the leader. Be a part of the team and you will someday lead the team yourself. I have always been honored to be the leader. I have to remind myself that the people downline are volunteers and can do what they want and that being their mentor or leader is a privilege not a right.

Michael Korda writing for Newsweek magazine wrote concerning "How to Be a Leader"... "At a moment when we are waiting to see whether we have elected a President or a leader, it is worth examining the differences between the two. For not every President is a leader, but every time we elect a President we hope for one, especially in times of doubt and crisis. In easy times we are ambivalent -- the leader, after all, makes demands, challenges the status quo, and shakes things up." Korda went on to say that "leaders are great simplifiers. They have a simple but eloquent message. People can only be led where they want to go. A leader must stir our blood, not appeal to our reason."

The Rotarians have a theme "Service above self." It would do us all good to remember that. The leader leads a public existence and is subjected to constant scrutiny. The decisions he or she makes will be examined and critiqued daily. The leader gives up many of the rights to be human. The pressures can be unbearable at times, but the real leader would have it no other way.

Success is built on inconvenience and leaders have to make accommodation for the life-style that goes along with the responsibilities of leadership. The rewards are such that in the context of the whole picture of life the benefits far out-weigh the downside. Living in a glass house of sorts can be tiring so you've got to watch yourself and take time for your family and friends as well as time away for yourself.

Bob Crisp - Raising a Giant 2.0

Note: I suggest when you go on "vacation" that you simply say you are "Out of town" it avoids some of the "while the cats away" syndrome.

The challenge of leadership is the challenge of excellence. Strive for excellence not perfection. When you make a mistake admit it! Learn from it and go on. Don't agonize or focus on what could have been but look ahead to what can be. Never let the past predict the future. Move ahead with boldness and confidence. By doing so you will discover that there is a large crowd following you.

The future is yours to do with whatever you please. Because you have chosen to be in network marketing, you have chosen to take some form of leadership role. It will likely expand with time and as your vision and responsibilities increase so will your rewards. My favorite motto was given to me on a key chain by a sales manager for a major hotel chain. It says,

"Make no small plans for they have no magic to stir men's blood."

People want leaders with vision and want to be led by people who are going somewhere important. Dream big, think big, and act big! Don't let small thinkers and critics govern your attitude and spirit.

Remember these words… "Leader of one… leader of many… if you can't lead one… you can't lead any."

The network marketing industry as a whole has always suffered from a disease I call "too much promise and too little delivered." It stems from the fact that so many people and companies get too caught up in making a fast buck that they forget the universal laws of success. They ignore the concept of always giving more than you promised.

Businesses built around the concept of ripping off the newcomers and taking advantage of the unknowing and naive don't last for long. Some of them however, rise to great sales heights only to plummet into the abyss overnight.

The really long-term deals may not appeal to the "get rich quick" crowd but they will appeal to those who value their reputation and want a lasting and fulfilling opportunity. One of the great things about network marketing is that it can provide for a certain degree of security as one grows older. Most network marketing businesses have provisions for retirement or "ambassador" status as well as allowing for businesses to be passed along to heirs and successors. Consider the longevity of a situation as well as the opportunity for immediate gain.

My first network marketing experience lasted for nine years and produced millions of dollars of income. When I was forced by the failure of other investments to liquidate my network marketing business I was able to sell my downline organization for a substantial sum of money. Not only did I create a substantial standard of living but I also accumulated a considerable net worth in my network marketing business.

The long term viability often rests in factors that you and I can't control, however, factors such as product quality, the management skills of the owners and employees, or outside government interference. We can, as independent business people, control many of the "field factors." By field factors I mean incremented training and business development programs that teach business skills as they are needed, and on an ever increasing and complex basis, leadership training.

Not everyone who comes into the business is ready to be full time. Most in fact are going to start out as part-timers with little real financial investment or personal commitment to the venture. The vast majority therefore have a built in back door. The participation in the decision making process may be limited but important.

When building honestly we must realize that training must be geared to bridging some reality gaps. Gaps that inevitably happen between the perceived success and the actual success of the participants. A new distributor who expected and often needed to make three thousand dollars in their third month but in fact only made three hundred dollars is in serious need of a shot of encouragement and some serious personal counseling and tutoring.

In more advanced development programs you must introduce people to the "A" player role and move them gradually into a more involved position of responsibility.

The advanced stages of training require much more thought and experience. My upline told me that until I had been in the business five years I wouldn't have any idea about the nature of the business I was in. I was incredulous! I couldn't believe that learning the business could be so complicated. It took me seven years before I could appreciate the wisdom of those words!

Wisdom is gained with experience. When you spend three years of your life building a leg of business that does millions of dollars of business and see it collapse in less than 30 days it can be pretty discouraging. When a divorce between your best leaders turns into a legal and acrimonious battle that is waged openly in front of their (and your) downlines you can lose a year's work overnight.

Advanced training programs should prepare you to deal with and identify problems before they become disasters. They should teach you how to avoid the predictable pitfalls of network marketing. In my advanced course on network marketing I spend most of my time on "counseling leaders," "reading problem areas before they get out of hand" and "preventing total disaster." With this knowledge alone I could have saved thousands of hours of work and untold hundreds of thousands of dollars not to mention the considerable stress and strain it put on me and my family.

Most companies focus on stage one. Not only do they focus on stage one they focus on part one of stage one. "Get them in and sell them some products." Their idea of a training program is teaching people to wear "the button," buy and use the products, and teach every one you sponsor to do "the same thing." This is great as far as it goes but having a successful business requires much more than simply wearing a button or filling your garage with thousands of dollars of products.

Being a success in network marketing requires years of training, nurturing and conditioning. The great news is that you can "earn while you learn." Many people earn large amounts of money while accessing knowledge for the stability and continued success of their business. The mistake so many make is believing that because they are making a substantial income that they suddenly know how to teach others to do it too. They wake up sometime in the future and discover they were not so knowledgeable and that a good deal of their success should have been credited to others or to a system or method they didn't develop but merely used.

Progress in network marketing takes time. Some people need basic communication skills, others need advanced training, and a majority needs to be immersed in a total make-over program. Personality traits differ, financial situations vary, and backgrounds are diverse in the extreme and yet most companies treat every new distributor the same. Often times distributors find their upline is unskilled or too busy to offer simple training and assistance to new members.

Politics become involved and deals are made which make defining leadership difficult if not entirely impossible. New companies are an amalgam of methods and training schemes and few have the courage or conviction to design a culture around sound people principles and business building techniques.

Strong businesses are built around programs not politics. People are treated as individuals and challenged to grow at their own pace. Nurturing and personal attention is a major part of the emphasis. Recognition is liberally dispensed and high pressure tactics are non-existent. Particular attention is paid to "keeping them in" so programs which develop personal confidence and self image are mingled with each event or event.

Bob Crisp - Raising a Giant 2.0

The incremental training programs never stop. Just as you must feed an adult a different diet than a child so must you feed a Giant in network marketing a larger and more diverse diet than the newcomer. It is a mistake to believe that anyone is a permanent fixture in your downline or upline. People's lives change as they get older. Children grow up and leave home.

Companies which offer serious training and leadership development programs find more of their people stay and become stabilizing factors. Credibility for long range goals is the norm. Doubters are quieted and continuity of leadership creates an atmosphere conducive to growth.

Leadership in today's world has been emasculated and made impotent by a media and government who treasure mediocrity and despise those who lead out. Consequently, good men and women are going undercover and holding back instead of stepping out and standing up. American leadership has been homogenized, mixed in with the crowd, the milk. In the past, the cream rose to the top. Today the cream gets blended in or skimmed off and discarded.

What we need are more people to step to the forefront and take the roles of leadership now held by those who abuse the privilege. We need men and women of principle who will ignore the criticism of the gossip hungry crowds and find the courage to be counted among the elite of history.

Michael Korda, former editor-in-chief of Simon and Schuster, said in an article in Newsweek magazine January

5, 1981 "A great leader must have a certain irrational quality, a stubborn refusal to face facts, infectious optimism, and the ability to convince us that all is not lost even when we're afraid it is. Confucius suggested that, while the advisors of a great leader should be as cold as ice, the leader himself should have fire, a spark of divine madness.

He won't come until we're ready for him, for the leader is like a mirror, reflecting back to us our own sense of purpose, putting into words our own dreams and hopes, transforming our needs and fears into coherent policies and programs."

Korda went on to say, "Our strength makes him strong; our determination makes him determined; our courage makes him a hero; he is, in the final analysis, the symbol of the best in us, shaped by our own spirit and will. And when these qualities are lacking in us, we cannot produce him; and even with all our skill at image building, we can't fake him. He is, after all, merely the sum of us."

Character and principle centered leadership will create programs for people which produce profits, instead of programs for profits which prey upon good people.

Chapter Eighteen
The Fall of A Giant and The Road Back

If you have made mistakes, even serious ones, there is always another chance for you. What we call failure is not the falling down, but the staying down. -- Mary Pickford

There are few things in life as devastating as having it all and losing it. I know, I scaled the mountain called success and fell from its lofty cliffs. It would be easy to claim it wasn't my fault. I didn't cause the price of oil to fall or the resulting value of my real estate holdings to collapse, but I did make the decisions which ultimately led to my own demise.

The seeds of defeat are sown long before the fall itself. When I elected to lead my very much "plugged in" network marketing organization down a more independent path, I set the course for the future leaders in my organization to do the same. When I elected to depart from the proven methods that had stood the test of time I eventually watered down the principles so that the message became muted and hard to define.

The ego is a powerful force and at a very young age I found myself the leader of a large and dynamic group of people. I was so influential in fact, as to be considered to be

Bob Crisp - Raising a Giant 2.0

a serious candidate for the United States Senate in my home state. I was feeling indestructible and ten feet tall. The downfall of the mighty can be found in their own success and certainly I was a willing victim.

I reached a six figure per month income in less than two years from the time I really got started in the network marketing business. My downline numbered in the tens of thousands and reached an apex of over two hundred thousand people! I owned several homes including a thirteen acre estate in the heart of Atlanta, Georgia. I had a 2.5 million dollar Cessna Citation II jet with two full time pilots to fly me anywhere at a moment's notice. I had a stable of cars including Rolls Royce's, Ferraris, Porsches, along with a liberal sprinkling of Mercedes, motorhomes and trucks. I owned an interest in a bank, hotels, automobile dealership, shopping center, and various other businesses and properties.

Everywhere I went a limousine picked me up and I stayed in the finest hotel suites. Politicians courted me and professional athletes and movie stars envied me. The world was my oyster and the sky was the limit. Then the sky caved in. In a matter of a few weeks, banks called notes and canceled lines of credit. My largest distributors led a revolt and fractured my once invincible group into thousands of fragments beyond repair. My income which had become substantial was cut in half and then in half again! Credit sources dried up and bankers refused to return calls.

Speaking engagements, once a source of inexhaustible income and pride, were canceled and overnight the world became a very dark place. I remember the final days when we were forced to leave our enormous home and watched as the trucks came and carried the luxury cars away. I remember a friend asking how I felt about losing it all. My reply was very simple and very sincere, "I started with nothing and built it once, I can do it again." Little did I realize how difficult it was going to be the second time around.

It all began with a difference of style I had with my upline leadership. I couldn't tolerate an emphasis that they had chosen to make that I felt was detrimental to the long term stability and growth of "my" organization. What I could not see and did not want to admit was that I was using this as an excuse to exercise my own ego. It comes down sometimes to control issues and I was ready, in my opinion, to be on my own.

What the impact was going to be was out of my scope of understanding. When counseling young up-and-comers today, I try to point out that it is not what you see or are aware of that kills you but what you don't see and are blinded to that is the killer. I know firsthand the destruction that can be wrought when the big "I" gets in the way.

The issue comes down to loyalty. Loyalty, fidelity, devotion, reverence, respect, regard, all are words that carry so much weight in network marketing. When loyalty breaks down in any organization the major ingredient of cohesion and continuity are missing the ingredient of trust. What I did not understand is that I had broken the trust between me and my upline. I had chosen a path of independence which would be soon duplicated by my own downline.

I taught and practiced the "THE Group" concept but eventually found I was more often practicing the "MY Group" concept. Even though I believed my reasons were pure and my intentions were honorable, I could not have done a worse thing for my own long term stability. When the chips were down and I needed loyalty from the ones closest to me I couldn't get it. The adage that "actions speak louder than words" is true.

I had built my entire life around the concept of helping others get what they wanted and I would get what I wanted. What I didn't want was to go from totally financially free to dead broke. Even at the top it wasn't the homes, cars or jets that impacted me most, but the success of others. However, I let my kingdom run me instead of running the kingdom. I let destiny shape my life instead of my life shaping my destiny.

I took something marvelous and wonderful and turned it into a nightmare - all because of my own ego. They say be kind to the people on the way up the ladder because they're the ones you'll meet on your way back down, but I went down so fast I couldn't see anyone.

Do you know what it's like to be totally broken? Not just hurt, but shattered? Do you know how it feels to sit alone in a dark room and stare at walls you can't see at 3 in the morning? I remember going for a run at 2 in the morning with a foot of snow on the ground because the tension was so great I couldn't stand to
lay in bed, and sleep was a thing of the distant past.

Do you know what it's like to have friends turn their back on you? To meet people on the street or in a restaurant who point their fingers at you and whisper behind your back "There's that guy that had it all and blew it"? I know all too well how that feels. I know how it feels to take my kids out of private schools, put them in a car and move them across the country to a strange new community, to a house smaller than our maids lived in before. It becomes difficult to look your son and daughters in the eyes and know that you have taken their security away. Oh, how sweet the success and how bitter the gall of defeat!

For years I had taught that one is not known by their successes alone but by what they do with their failures and I determined that I was going to come back, that I would never let the circumstances get me down. I subscribe basically to the theory that after the age of adulthood there simply aren't any victims only volunteers and I wasn't going to be a volunteer for failure.

I soon realized the talents and determination that had led me up the ladder were still intact and that though I was fifteen years older now the road back was still available. I began again. I made new friends and began to mend fences with old ones. I ate a lot of crow during the first few months and even now find a dish being shoved my way occasionally. It is not one of the finer delicacies of life but it never made anyone sick to eat every now and again.

I realized that it was my spiritual life that gave me the strength to go on during the darkest hours and that the concepts and precepts of success were ingrained in me. All the books and CDs, seminars and events had made a lasting impression and would be the foundation on which I would build again.

Bob Crisp - Raising a Giant 2.0

Many friends have helped along the way. My two best friends… Pat Yamada and Dr. Vince Thomas and his wife Diana, Pamela Berryhill, Bill Gonzales (now deceased such a shame to lose a good friend so early), Dexter Yager who spared no rod in beating some lessons into a young, arrogant student, the patience of Rick Setzer, best-selling author and friend Denis Waitley, friend and mentor Jim Rohn and so many more..

Someone has said that the beauty of America is in the opportunity to begin again-to be down and to get back up, to be out and be allowed the chance to get back in, to be rich, poor, and rich again. But it takes patience and determination, and an iron will to get off the canvas after being dealt a blow and come up swinging haymakers.

For many years I flew like a young eagle that rested on a lofty mountain top at night and soared during the day. Then came the flight over water, no islands in the sun, no lofty perches to rest my wings, no fellow travelers to share the way or hear my song. Today I search for the "final island in the sun" the home where eagles go to meet and to encourage one another. Once again I feel the long and winding road of success calling. The desire to go is stronger than the urge to stay. To take one more shot at the top of the mountain and to risk failure in search of success is the call of the free, a call so certain I would never dare refuse.

You're reading this book and so I can assume you have decided to make the trip too. I look forward to eventually meeting you on that road for it is a road worth taking.   If you have just begun your journey or if you have been on the road for as many years as me, don't turn back! Someone may be using your tracks.

BOB CRISP - RAISING A GIANT 2.0

To all of the many unknown friends who have said a prayer for me along the way or shook my hand or said a kind word I want thank you and offer you whatever encouragement you may need today. I truly believe without each other we are impotent. Know that no matter how long or how tough your journey may have been or may be that in a small village on the sea in Southern California there is an old eagle with one more flight in him who will be out there paying the price with you everyday.

Don't let the turkeys get you down. Soar with the eagles instead. And don't let anyone steal your dream! I've always loved the thoughts expressed by this piece sent to me some twenty years ago and hope you will find the sentiment helpful too.

"I will persist until I succeed. I was not delivered unto this world in defeat, nor does failure course in my veins. I am not a sheep waiting to be prodded by my shepherd. I am a lion and I refuse to talk, to walk, to sleep with the sheep. I will hear not those who weep and complain, for their disease is contagious. Let them join the sheep. The slaughterhouse of failure is not my destiny."
                                                              __ Anonymous

CONTACT ME

To contact me for speaking engagements or personal coaching go to www.gobobcrisp.com or read my weekly blog at www.gocrispblog.com or check out the best tool for recruiting there ever was www.allaxismedia.com (disclosure this is my company and is NOT a network marketing company)

I prefer to communicate via email. If you send me an email I will find the time to answer you as soon as possible. My email addresses are bob@allaxismedia.com or bobcrisp212@yahoo.com

THANK YOU

I want to say thank you to so many people who have meant so much to me along the way. To enumerate all the remarkable people and their contributions to my life would be impossible here. Vince and Diana Thomas, Pat Yamada, Roger and Cathy Blake, Joni Locht, Adam Packard, Joe Cutler, Carsten Werner and his wife Ingrid, my children Candace her husband Jason, Julie, and Jeremy and his gorgeous new wife Tammy and so many legendary figures from the network marketing world.

Thanks to Tom Chenault for having me on his radio program.

Thanks to Dexter Yager's "spare no rod" attitude toward an impertinent young leader... I finally learned the lessons of leadership... thanks to Rick Setzer's patience, Bill Britt's firm hand and encouragement I just couldn't quit... and Rich DeVos the co-founder of Amway and a man I still consider to be a second father... he taught me how to be a man. All have contributed so much to my success.

Thanks to you all and so many more of you who have bought my books and said so many good things... thanks for the edits too.

And remember these words... "He that walketh with the wise, grows wise" Please, if you liked this book... tell others about my "Stuff" today... thanks.